ALASKA RAILROAD

NORTHBOUND PASSENGER TRAIN with the Pyramids, 5500 ft./1677 m.
high, in the backbround; M.P.-342.7.

ALASKA RAILROAD

THE GREAT DENALI TREK
VOLUME I

BY NICHOLAS DEELY

SUNDANCE
Books

FRONT COVER: Northbound passenger train at the north end of Broad Pass, passing below Mt. Denali, 20,320 ft./6195 m. high, 60 mi./100 km. away.

BACK COVER: HOLLAND AMERICA LINE, Westours, full length dome car passing in front of Mt. Denali.

ALASKA RAILROAD

VOLUME I

SUNDANCE PUBLICATIONS *Ltd.*

250 BROADWAY, DENVER, COLORADO 80203

Published by
Sundance Publications, Ltd., Denver, Colorado

Graphical Presentation and Printing by
Sundance Publications, Ltd., Denver, Colorado

Binding by
Schaffer Bindery, Magna, Utah

Typesetting by
Silverton Standard, Silverton Colorado

Editing by - Steven J. Meyers
Production Manager - Dell A. McCoy
Photographic Director - Steven J. Meyers

ISBN   0-913582-46-8

NORTHBOUND PASSENGER TRAIN in Healy
Canyon; M.P.-352.7.

Dedicated to:

The Railroaders, everywhere,

for

in the pursuit of trains, I have come to

know and love the peoples of the World

Acknowledgments

One's accomplishments do not necessarily represent a result of a singular effort, but rather the sum total effort of a multitude of inter-reacting forces, human and otherwise. To this end, I owe a great deal of gratitude to the following people who were instrumental in providing these forces and assets:

BERNICE, my loving wife who has continuously, throughout our marriage supported me and offered the encouragement to mold my dreams into a reality; who long ago recognized that the pursuit of trains, and exploration of the wilderness was my medicine to myself, and who always wished me "Bon Voyage" when I left on these treks, and waited, whatever the hour, for my safe and happy return.

HANS KARL REX, Geologist, Engineer, and owner of Alaska International Models, and KEITH MEREDITH, Captain, U.S.A.F., my frequent companions into the wilderness, to places so remote that one would not venture out on his own. To those memories of hot coffee and cinnamon rolls along the trail, which have never tasted so good, and sadly never will again. To a comraderie that became indelible, only to suddenly crash, like a story from a Greek tragedy, with the untimely demise of our beloved friend, HANS.

K.A. SMITH, Terminal Superintendent, Fairbanks, Alaska Railroad, without whose efforts and assistance this narrative could not have been written. To the countless enjoyable hours spent in his office and along the line, while all these facts were put forth in straight forward descriptive railroad language.

MERLIN PARKER, General Yard Master, Fairbanks, and ELI CRAYTON, and LINDA HARRELSON, Station Agents, Healy, for their kindness and service with courtesy, when providing me, so many times, with a daily schedule of train movements. Without their help this project would have been futile.

STEVEN LOVE, Roadmaster, GORDAN DUVELL, Yard Master, Fairbanks, and so many other Alaska Railroad employees who were so helpful, in so many ways.

PATRICIA ELAM, my faithful, then pregnant, nurse, who scheduled my pediatric patients at the Healy Clinic so as not to conflict with train movements; who tiptoed through the snow with me during those clinics in search of that ultimate railroad picture.

JODY MEREDITH, who admonished me for writing and spelling phonetically in concert with my Yankee New England accent. She thus offered to translate and correct my narrative, so that I might be able to communicate with other English speaking peoples.

REX RUNDQUIST, fellow physician and friend, who graciously lent me that use of his library and covered the medical service periodically, so that I might pursue this endeavor.

VINCENT HANEMAN, Dean, School of Engineering, RONALD GATTERDAM, Professor of Computer Science, both at the University of Alaska and RON YOUNG, Construction Engineer, and the members of the TANANA VALLEY MODEL RAILROAD CLUB, who spent their valuable time critiquing my slides and offering candid, constructive criticism.

JAMES V. DREW, Dean, School of Agriculture and Land Resources, Management, University of Alaska, for providing the needed material for the text on the University and Agriculture.

DWIGHT DEELY, Educator, BETTY ALDERTON, and MARY ROEHM, who deciphered my handwritten notes to form a cohesive typewritten manuscript. This was carried out with such adroitness, that I have lost my fears of illiteracy.

RICK REDICK, Graphic Artist, who worked so hard to produce the maps and sketches for this text.

Finally, to those wonderful girls at the FAIRBANKS CLINIC, RO HOOTEN, RHONDA YOUNG, and CHERYL HELLICKSON, who upon request were so kind to type up those bits and pieces that ultimately bound this volume together.

THANK YOU ALL.

Bibliography

1. Davis, Neil. **Alaska Science Nuggets**. Fairbanks, Alaska: University of Alaska, Geophysical Institute, 1982.

2. Williams, Howel. **Landscapes of Alaska**. University of California Press.

3. Heacox, Kim. **Denali Road Guide**. Alaska Natural History Association, 1986.

4. Simmerman, Nancy Lange. **Alaska's Parklands**. The Mountaineers, Seattle.

5. Sierra Club. **The Sierra Club Guides to the National Parks of the Pacific Northwest and Alaska**. Random House.

6. Clifford, Howard. **Rails North**. Seattle: Superior Publishing Co.

7. Brovald, Ken C. **Alaska Wilderness Rails**. Missoula, Montana: Pictorial Histories Publishing Company.

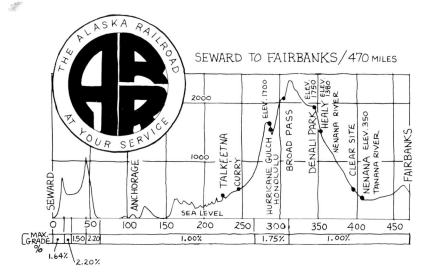

Foreword

While traveling on the Furka-Oberalp Railway in Switzerland several years ago, a German acquaintance asked me as we admired the ascending ride from Andermatt, how the Alps compared with the Alaska Range. I pondered for a short while, considering his query, when suddenly he answered the question himself, stating, "They are of a different character."

This immediately ignited a flashback to my university days when I first dreamed of Alaska. Every possible source of photographic information was addressed. Many beautiful photographs were received from various Alaskans, but somehow what I had envisioned was not there.

Upon arriving in Alaska, my suppositions were immediately confirmed. I saw the mountains of the Alaska Range far differently than others. They are an entity in their own right and are of a different character; for indeed, they can only be superficially compared to their counterparts. This is a sub-arctic, living WILDERNESS still in its genesis.

Paradoxically, they are not as high as other ranges. Yet individually and discreetly apart they are much higher, piercing the sky like isolated church spires. These behemoths at 12,000ft/3658m, 14000ft/4268m, 17000ft/5182m are ultimately overshadowed by "the great one", Mount Denali at 20,320ft/6195m. Where other ranges are speckled with lakes, this range is crowded with extensive glaciers fed from snowfalls, with accumulation less than their counterparts elsewhere. Finally, the uniqueness and character of this range can best be understood when one realizes it is the most rugged and inhospitable mountain barrier in the world.

The Alaska Railroad, falling in the shadow of this great group of mountains, reflects its own unmistakable character. I am hopeful, therefore, that I might be able to share with the reader, through my photography, the same feeling of ectasy that I have of the living earth, and man with his machine.

Introduction

A railroad is not just a flanged wheel rolling on a ribbon of steel. It is a reaction between its physical properties, man, and most importantly, the environment. By understanding the natural and human factors that compose this whole picture, it is hoped that the reader will have a greater sense of appreciation of the forces contributing to these scenes. The unparalleled beauty of the right-of-way is the catalyst that sets the environmental intrigue into motion. Accordingly, this material is presented in a format of a travelogue. In this manner, all these facets will be interwoven, including as much scientific and technical detail as possible, to form a narrative visualization of each scene as it unfolds.

KEITH MEREDITH, kneeling and Hans Rex standing at Honolulu hair-pin curve, M.P.-288.7. Both were frequent companions into remote and dangerous sections of the line.

CLOSE-UP OF THE LATE HANS REX, teacher, companion and friend. Without the companionship and security (so necessary in the dangerous bush) provided both by Hans Rex and Keith Meredith, this book might not have been written. Photo by Keith Meredith.

To photograph this material represented extreme joy, coupled with great fatigue, stress, and fear. As Hans Rex, a frequent close companion stated, while up to his shoulders in snow, "If only the photography could portray the effort that went into getting these shots." Initially, there was the concern for bear and moose. Since one can shoot only with a camera in the Denali National Park, courage and cowardice played a simultaneous role. One had to contend with blizzards, rain and ice-cold glacier fed streams. In the hot summers, it was the mosquitoes and black flies of the tundra that tortured the flesh with each trek into the bush. Many pictures were taken from ledges and rock outcroppings of questionable stability. More than once I felt the ledge giving way. But, more frightning is when ledges and loose rocks above you come plummeting down. The Nenana River Canyon, with its sedimentary and metamorphic rock walls, particularly, caused numerous palpitations. As can be seen, the railroad doesn't fare much better. This is strikingly evident by the numerous cribbings and steel abutments needed to prevent the track from sliding down into the canyon. Because of the general wilderness character of the Alaska Railroad, in conjunction with the joys, but also the great difficulties this enumerated, I elected to concentrate in Volume I, of this presentation on that portion of the line north of Talkeetna. In this sense, it truly falls in the shadow of Mount Denali.

In the same regard, the reader will note that the name Mount McKinley will be mentioned only once in this book, which is at this point for purposes of clarification. We Alaskans refer to the most dominant mountain on the North American continent in the context of the cultural and ethnic origins of our state. So in concert with our Native American Alaskans, we too, look upon this goliath as MOUNT DENALI, "The Great One". It is the official name given to this mountain by the State of Alaska. And now, through the medium of this photography and narrative, have a nice trip!

Unless otherwise specified,
photographs are taken
by the author.

AUTHOR ENDURING a long wait—patiently, in extreme cold—for the arrival of the northbound OWL freight train. Photo by Keith Meredith.

Biography

Nicholas Deely was born in Lawrence, Massachusetts. Subsequently, he was raised both in Massachusetts and New Hampshire and considers both states his childhood home. Prior to his university education, he served in the U.S. Navy, aboard ship, in the South Pacific. Originally a high school teacher, he eventually became a physician specializing in children's diseases.

His interest in trains has been life-long. How and why this fascination developed is unknown. As a boy he remembers spending many enjoyable evenings watching Boston and Maine trains passing through Exeter, New Hampshire. In later years, the thrill of New England mountain railroading could be observed just by looking out of the bedroom window, in Bartlett, New Hampshire. Maine Central freights would attach their helper units to the rear of the train and then charge up through spectacular Crawford Notch on their way, ultimately, to Montreal.

Shortly after finishing his medical training at the Montreal Children's Hospital, a teaching unit of McGill University, Montreal, Canada, he and his family left for Alaska. "To be needed" was the philosophical emphasis in his re-location. He became the first Pediatrician in Fairbanks, which serves an area larger than the state of Texas. His arrival led to a relationship with the Fairbanks Clinic which continues today after 25 years.

His love for Alaska with its unparalleled beauty and his continued fascination with trains ultimately led to the development of this book, the first of two volumes. The presentation of this topic in a rather unique format caused his daughter, Bonnie Jean, to remark, "The book 'could be' a beautiful presentation of scenic Alaska, only the train happens to be in it." The author is hopeful that he has accomplished his goal.

THE AUTHOR on a small trestle 1 mi./1.6 km. north of Hurricane. Photo by Keith Meredith.

**SOUTHBOUND FREIGHT entering the north end of Broad Pass. M.P..317.
Alaska range in the background.**

LOOKING TO THE EAST; a northbound passenger train crossing Riley Creek trestle, Denali National Park; M.P.-347.7. Photo by Scott Hunter Deely.

TABLE OF CONTENTS

SOUTHBOUND FREIGHT TRAIN passing drying fish, Indian style, Nenana; M.P.-411.7.

A BRIEF HISTORY

Chapter **I**

DALL
SHEEP

Indians and Eskimos of Alaska claim through their mythology to be descendants of the raven, or of many other creatures of the northern wilderness. Through the years, these people have been influenced by another "animal" emigrating from the south. This "animal" is the Iron Horse, and its people have become known as Alaskan Railroaders. The persistent and everchanging adversities of this land, together with the great distance from immediate assistance and source of supplies, have created a resourcefulness and muted pride in both these people. Situated closer to Russia than the continental United States, 471mi/785km of standard-gauge main-line track treads northward into a primeval adventure of superlatives. From temperate coastal Seward, situated at approximately 60 degrees N. latitude, the line transverses three mountain ranges to reach its northern terminus, sub-arctic Fairbanks, 120mi/200km south of the Arctic Circle, and just below the 65th N. parallel. It geographically corresponds roughly to Oslo, Norway, and Helsinki, Finland, on the Seward end of the line, and Arkhagel'sk Russia, on the Fairbanks end. Although this is the northern-most railroad in North America, the Norwegian State Railways penetrate the arctic at Bod and Narvik, and the Soviet Railways at Murmansk.

Gold, the catalyst that lures men to ends of the earth, precipitated the need for the construction of the Alaska Railroad. Seeking an all-American route to the gold fields, the Alaska Central Railroad Company was established in 1902. This was one of three railroads that led ultimately to the establishment of the Alaska Railroad as we know it today.

Starting at Seward, the standard-gauge line extended 51 mi/85km north, to the Kenai peninsula before falling into receivership in 1909. A reorganization of the company took place to form a new entity, the Alaska Northern Railroad Company. Track was now extended to Kern Creek up along the Turnagain Arm. This represented a further extension of the original Alaska Central Railroad of 21mi/35km, for a total of 71mi/118km. From this point, on the Turnagain Arm, boats would carry supplies to the origins of the Iditarod Trail, on Knik Arm, which served as a travel and supply route to western Alaska's gold fields.

Financial crisis hit this new company in 1915. Further intervention, this time by the United States government, resulted in the purchase of the physical assets of the Alaska Northern Railway. The line was now known as the U.S. Government Railroad. Shortly after this acquisition, the headquarters of the line was shifted from Seward to Ship Creek, later to be renamed Anchorage.

Construction of the line, after many delays, was re-established, pushing it north by 1921 to an Indian village on the Tanana River now known as Nenana. This community was, and still is, the distribution point by barge for freight down the Tanana River to the world famous Yukon River. Traveling both upstream and downstream this passage eastward leads to the Yukon Territory of Canada and westward to the Bering Sea of the Pacific Ocean.

While all this construction was going on, the three foot narrow-gauge Tanana Valley Railroad was taken over in 1917 by the Alaska Railroad Commission. This led to an incorporation with the newly formed U.S. Government Railroad. While the Tanana Valley Railroad primarily served Fairbanks and the surrounding gold fields, it was eventually extended down to the Tanana River, just across from Nenana. Here, a unique winter operation developed whereby track was laid temporarily across the ice for about a quarter of a mile to reach Nenana on the other side. This then provided a means for the transport of winter freight. In the summer, freight was reloaded onto barges from the narrow-gauge cars, on the north shore of the Tanana River, to be transfered by water to the other side.

By 1923, the bridge across the Tanana River was completed linking both sections of the line. This structure, known as the Mears Memorial Bridge, is a 700ft/213.4km long single truss structure, making it one of the longest spans of the type in the world. The narrow-gauge line to Fairbanks was converted to standard-gauge, opening the door for an all-rail transit from the coast to Fairbanks and into the Golden North.

Except for the addition and subsequent deletion of several branch lines, this is now the railroad as we know it today. The most important of these additions was the Whittier Cut-off built in 1942-1943. With this completion, the Alaska Railroad now had two ice-free ports, Seward and Whittier. On July 15th, 1923, the Golden Spike was driven on the north end of the Tanana River by President Warren G. Harding, completing the 471 mile/7854km railroad now known as the Alaska Railroad. The line remained an operation of the United States Department of Interior until January 5th, 1985. On this momentous date, at Nenena, the Alaska Railroad was transferred from the United States Department of Interior to the State of Alaska. At last, it was now an Alaskan operation.

15

DALL SHEEP near railroad, Denali National Park.

DOG TEAM PASSING RDC in Nenana; M.P.-411.7. Musher Doug Bowers.
Mother in sled, Kathy Lenniger. Child, Lucas Bowers.

SOUTHBOUND COAL TRAIN at Windy; M.P.-326.7. Mt. Panorama, 6000 ft./ 1829 m. high in the background.

18

Chapter II

BROWN
BEAR

THE LINE

Total mileage of the Alaska Railroad is 650 mi/1083 km. Of this, 471mi/785km is mainline. The other 180mi/300km consists of branches, sidings, and terminal track. The 12.4mi/20.6km branch to Whittier from Portage, M.P.-64.2 is in fact a second mainline. While the Seward mainline goes over the mountain, the branch to the seaport of Whittier burrows under the Chugach Mountains. Approximately 4.3mi/7.1km from Portage, this line enters Portage tunnel, 0.95mi/1.58km long. Emerging from the east portal a 238ft/72.1m trestle is crossed. It then hugs the shore of glacier filled Portage Lake to enter, 1mi/1.6km away, Whittier tunnel 2.52mi/4.2km long. Enroute between the tunnels the line passes through Bear Valley, the home of the Williwaws. These are the fierce winds that howl down through this valley, at right angles to the railroad, to topple railroad cars right off the tracks. After passing through the latter tunnel the line comes into Prince William Sound and ultimately to the port of Whittier.

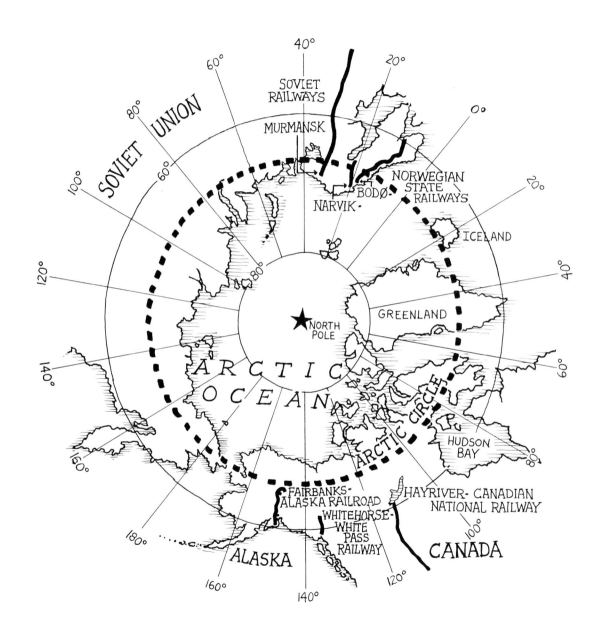

40°

SOVIET
RAILWAYS

20°

0°

60°

80°

SOVIET UNION

MURMANSK

60°

NORWEGIAN
STATE
RAILWAYS

100°

BODØ·

NARVIK·

20°

60°

ICELAND

120°

80°

40°

★ NORTH
POLE

GREENLAND

140°

60°

A R C T I C
O C E A N

ARCTIC CIRCLE

HUDSON
BAY

80°

160°

FAIRBANKS-
ALASKA RAILROAD

HAYRIVER- CANADIAN
NATIONAL RAILWAY

100°

180°

WHITEHORSE-
WHITE
PASS
RAILWAY

CANADA

ALASKA

160°

120°

140°

Further north is the Palmer branch 6.5mi/10.8km long. It branches off from the mainline at Matanuska Jct., M.P.-157, and has heavy movements of gravel trains. Originally it extended to the coal mines of Eska and Jonesville. This segment of the line has been abandoned. Now, Healy, M.P.-358.7, is the origin of all coal movements. Here too, the original coal hauling branch is no longer used, but is still intact. It is 4.7mi/7.8km long. All coal is loaded at Usibelli Tipple, M.P.-362.3 located on a spur just off the mainline. Coal is loaded into the hopper cars from the tipple while the train passes under it, at a continuous speed of 3 m.p.h./5 kph. From Fairbanks the longest branch of them all heads in a southeasterly direction to North Pole and Eielson Air Force Base. It is at this location, near a far corner of the base, that the end of steel for the Alaska Railroad really ends. It is 23mi/38.3km long. New 115lb./52.2kg rail has recently been laid to service the oil refinery at North Pole, and the military at Eielson. Valdez, a coastal community on Prince William Sound, had the most unique branch of the whole system. It is detached by hundreds of miles from the Alaskan Railroad, yet it had a modest railroad yard. Track was not laid in the conventional manner, but put down in sections like a toy model electric railroad set. Barges delivered freight cars loaded with pipeline construction materials to the dock, to be unloaded by a small track-mobile. This occurred during the construction of the Alaska pipeline during the 1970s. Freight was subsequently distributed by truck up along the pipeline route. Presently, the yard is abandoned.

TRACK:

Mainline track is laid and maintained to the highest standards possible. Rail is 39ft/12m long and 115lbs/52kg to the yard/meter. It is laid on creosoted wooden ties on a ballasted base of rock and gravel. At Montana Creek, M.P.-209.3, there is a short section of track which has been laid, for experimental purposes, only, on concrete ties. No welded rail exists at the present time. On curves, the outside rail is elevated and held in place with special clips and plates known as Pandrol. For smoothness of ride, it almost approximates that of welded track.

At all mainline switches a special device known as a "moose lock" has been installed. Since moose, unfortunately, represent a source of frequent head-on encounters along the line, it has been named after them. Its purpose is to keep the switch locked in its fixed position at all times should a foreign object, moose, or otherwise, strike and detach the switch stand. The resulting open switch would cause obviously, a derailment of the train.

21

NORTHBOUND PASSENGER TRAIN along the frozen Nenana River at M.P. 335. Un-named peak in the background.

OPERATIONS

Tides, basically, determine train movements, for incoming barges are unloaded at high tide. Since the line has no other railroad connection, these water carriers act as the intermediary leg for freight coming in from various origins. Prince Rupert, British Columbia, a Canadian National Railway connection, serves as one of these points. Loaded railroad freight cars travel by barge from here to Whittier, a distance of 790mi/1317km. Each barge has a capacity of 60 cars. Other freight from rail and truck origins is dispatched from Seattle, Washington, via barge to Whittier, 1378mi/2296.6km, to Seward 1234mi/2057km, and to Anchorage 1428mi/2380km. Included in this freight is considerable TOFC (Trailer on Flat Car) and COFC (Container on Flat Car). Additional freight consists of coal, gravel, and petroleum which represents (with TOFC/COFC) ninety percent of freight traffic. In addition, increasing oil exploration has initiated increased pipe shipments. Considerable local freight also makes up a reasonable portion of the total tonnage. This is destined for the river port of Nenana. From here, river barges transport this cargo, during the summer months, to the numerous villages along the Yukon River. All trains along the entire line are dispatched and controlled from Anchorage using a system known as Traffic Warrent Control. Locally, this is known as poor man's C.T.C.

TRAIN MOVEMENTS—FREIGHT

Coal, an increasing freight commodity, originates in Healy and is destined both for local use, and for export. Overseas shipments go to Korea, with experimental shipments, presently, to Taiwan. Korean bound coal travels in a unit train consisting of 65 cars, each car of 80 ton capacity. Trains depart Healy three times a week for Seward where coal is stockpiled for ultimate shipment to Asia. Northbound coal trains from Healy to Fairbanks vary in frequency from 2 to 5 times per week, destined for local use in Clear Air Force station, Fairbanks, and Eielson Air Force Base, 23mi/38.3km beyond the "end of the line".

Gravel is mined in Palmer area and shipped via the 6.5mi/10.8km Palmer-Matanuska branch to Anchorage. Local ordinances prevent gravel mining in the Anchorage area, and with ever-increasing construction in the community, the need for a constant delivery of gravel became paramount. As a result, from what was a dormant branch, two to eight, 80-car unit trains a day, pound these rails on their way to Anchorage, 42.9mi/71.5km away.

Petroleum is the latest addition to unit rail travel. Refineries in North Pole, a suburb of Fairbanks, process

north slope crude into various specialty products for use in Fairbanks and Anchorage. Daily freight trains contain extensive strings of tank cars, either as a unit train, or in a mixed tonnage consist. Thus, a reciprocal exchange of varied petroleum products exists between the states two largest communities, to be used exclusively by Alaskans.

TOFC/COFC transport represent a considerable amount of the freight carried by the railroad. It arrives, via barge, to one of Alaska's two ice free ports, Seward and Whittier, and is then loaded on specially designed articulated flat cars composed of three permanently coupled units. There are a total of forty-five of these units suitable for this type of cargo. Overnight service is guaranteed between Alaska's two largest cities, Anchorage and Fairbanks.

PASSENGER SERVICE

From the last of May to mid-September the increasingly popular daily passenger service between Anchorage and Fairbanks is in operation. It traverses this 356mi/593km route in 11 hours which challenges the Glacier Express of Switzerland's famous Rhatische Bahn as the "slowest express train in the world". However, the purpose of the trip is not just getting there, but the experience of getting there. All trains stop at Denali National Park where most passengers detrain. Their place is quickly taken by another group finishing the next leg of the trip. In comparison, few passengers travel the full length of this trip in one day.

In addition to the usual number of coaches, a dome car and a dining car, the train usually has four or five private tour cars. These are operated by Holland/American Line—Westours Line, and Princess Tours—Alaska Tours. The cars are full-length, double-decked, and glass-domed. Besides having the benefit of a 360 degree horizontal view, there is a celestial 180 degree view. The upper level seats 60 passengers, while the lower level of each houses a kitchen and dining room. Indeed, this train represents an uncommon luxury amidst a wilderness of uncommon beauty.

Additional summer passenger transportation consists of a local "bush" service from Anchorage to Hurricane Gulch bridge on Wednesdays, with a return the same day. On Saturdays the same train, a RDC, Budd car(s) makes the same trip, going all the way to Denali National Park. It returns to Anchorage on Sunday. The train stops anywhere along the line at the request of the passengers. Riders on this run usually consist of adventurers tramping

CARIBOU

SOUTHBOUND PASSENGER TRAIN crossing trestle on the south face of Mt. Healy.

SOUTHBOUND PASSENGER TRAIN, north end of Healy Canyon.

THE GREAT DENALI TREK

out into the bush, homesteaders returning to the solitude of their life style along the isolated rail line, sportsmen, and those who seek a leisurely passage through this superlative wilderness.

The winter schedule consists, usually, of a singular RDC between Anchorage and Fairbanks scheduled for each weekend. On a mid-week schedule the same train goes only as far as the middle of Hurricane Gulch bridge and then returns to Anchorage the same day. These trains are primarily a local service for those folks along an isolated stretch of the line seeking an access to the rest of Alaska. However, there is an increasing off-season tourist patronage to explore Alaska's winter wonderland.

What seemed to have been lost forever has now risen like a Phoenix from the ashes of yesterday. It is the 114.3mi/190.5km trip from Anchorage to Seward. Many years ago passenger service to Seward was terminated. Presently, however, service is offered three days a week during the summer months. What unfolds is at least an equal counterpart of the northern run. With no apologies to anyone, this truly is one of the most beautiful

wilderness railroad trips in the world.

Whittier serves not only as an important port for the Alaska Railroad, but also as an important port for the State of Alaska ferry system. It is also a mecca for the sportsman, the sailor, and the adventurer who seeks the grandest display of coastal glaciers in the world. From Portage, M.P.-64.2 on the mainline, the 12.4mi/20.6km branch line goes on to this port. Since there is no road access to this community, the railroad acts as a conduit for the passengers and motor vehicles to and from Portage and Whittier. To a variable degree, passenger service is maintained both summer and winter, with some runs starting in Anchorage. Usually there is a locomotive, several passenger cars, and a string of specially reconstructed flatcars for vehicle transport. Uniquely, because of this isolation, Whittier's ambulance service uses the railroad to transport, at least to Portage, emergency medical care enroute to Anchorage. A conventional ambulance is fitted with a set of flanged wheels, in addition to conventional tires, to be raised or lowered for rail service as the situation requires.

TRACK GANG, "speeder" northbound, Healy Canyon, near Healy; M.P.-358.7.

Chapter IV

ENVIRONMENTAL MAINTENANCE

Beyond all measurement the "Great Spirit" that brings the beauty and greatness to this land, brings also its wrath. Virtually all the great obstacles to effective railroad operations seem to fall upon this line. Tucked between operations of the trains and the constant vigilance needed to keep them running is a situation whose contradiction is total.

Frost heaves cause the track to buckle upwards, while melting ice results in the downward sag of the line. The result is a spaghetti-like track. Since this is an annual repair operation, tracks shimming can, perhaps, be considered a normal routine operating procedure.

Floods also represent an annual ritual somewhere along the line. Heavy rains turn creeks into savage flows, that destroy all in their path. The most recent incident of this force was demonstrated on October 13, 1986 when the normally placid Montana Creek, M.P.-209.3, tore out the railroad bridge and a large segment of the line.

Another annual event occurs in the spring when the rivers break their bondage of ice. Resulting ice flows cause jams, or ice dams, which can force rivers in such a direction as to place the railroad in harms way.

Earthquakes are common in Alaska, but fortunately, they are usually mild. Immediate inspection of the line becomes mandatory and routine. However, on Good Friday, March 27, 1964, the routine inspection following an earthquake measuring 8.4 on the Richter Scale, could be done with a cursory glance. The railroad was gone! Portage, M.P.-64.2 had sunk 12ft/3.6m to bring it below sea level. Tracks and bridges were destroyed and under water. The parallel highway suffered the same fate.

Train movements, once the track was repaired, was possible only at LOW TIDE. Seward yard no longer existed, having gone out to sea. The same destruction also was present in parts of Anchorage. The Alaska Railroad, with the same defiance that was exhibited by all Alaskans affected by this unexpected early "break-up", rebuilt the railroad. It has never looked back, but continues to forge ahead in every aspect of its system.

Temperature extremes, 90 degrees F/32 degrees C to -60 degrees F/-52 degrees C play tricks with the physical plant as well as with human efficiency. Steel becomes brittle, motive power ratings decrease, cars and trains move sluggishly. Any break down at these low temperatures can be a major catastrophe, and very dangerous. Summer warmth brings relief to the track crews. By the same token, swarms of mosquitos and black flies nourish in this seasonal change to torment everything, work crews and animals alike.

Snow as a problem is to be expected in Alaska, but, as one goes further north, the amount of precipitation **diminishes**. The regions about Whittier, M.P.-12.4, Grand View, M.P.-44.9, and Moose Pass, M.P.-29.3 may accumulate as much as 25ft/7.7m of snow. Talkeetna, M.P.-226.7, which is further north, but south of the Alaska Range, measures accumulations of 15ft/4.5m. Fairbanks, 120mi/200km south of the Arctic Circle can expect a seasonal fall of about 5ft/1.5m. The snow fleet, stationed in Anchorage, responds to existing snow storms, as needed, anywhere along the line. The fleet consists of rotary snowplows, Jordan spreaders and snow plows permanently fixed to the front end of all locomotives.

Paradoxically, what presents the biggest problem to the railroad is not the snow accumulation; but rather, the results of plowing. What is now an easy route for the trains to transverse, becomes also an easy route for the Moose. What is created is actually a "moat" and thus an obstacle to the free movement of the moose beyond the track. The consequence is usually the death of the moose during any encounter with a train. Three hundred and sixteen moose were killed by trains during the winter of 1984-85. Fortunately, in the following years the number of kills has decreased. Now, an even greater menace has come upon the scene, the "snowgoers". Where human logic would tell them otherwise, these snowgoers use "moose logic" and head down the railroad right-of-way with no knowledge of train movements. Fortunately, there have been no fatalities, yet!

FIREWEED

FERRY; M.P.-371.2. Southbound passenger train having just passed over the Nenana River. Note "spikes" between the rails to prevent automobiles from using the railroad bridge.

CLEARING OUT "GLACIER ICE" at M.P.-336. Steven Love, Roadmaster in the foreground.

SHIMMING OF UNEVEN TRACK caused by frost heaves and melting perma-frost.

GLACIER MELTING UNIT with 50 gallon double open-ended drum submerged in the ice and filled with burning charcoal and salt. Note hanging electrical outlet for supplemental ice melting facility via the radiation of heat created by an electrical filament.

SOUTHBOUND PASSENGER TRAIN hitting snow bluff. Alaska range in the background.

EXAMPLE OF STEEL BEAMS interlaced with steel cables needed to hold sections of the roadbed together.

ANOTHER EXAMPLE of structural support for the roadbed; "million dollar curve."

32   **SOUTHBOUND PASSENGER TRAIN passing over "million dollar curve." M.P.-351.**

WORK TRAIN near unnamed lake, north end of Broad Pass. Talkeetna
mountains in the background.

GREG PARKER grinding rail at M.P.-321. K.A. Smith, Terminal Superintendent, Fairbanks, looking on.

SECTION CREW cleaning switch south of Windy, M.P.-324.7.

K.A. SMITH, Terminal superintendent Fairbanks, in the trackmobile talking with Steven Love, Road-master, about track conditions further down the line. Location, Oliver; M.P.-342.7. Sugarloaf Mountain in the background.

WORK TRAIN; M.P.-336. Hi-rail inspection car and Alaska range in the background.

RDC PASSING OVER newly formed glacier ice located under the small bridge
and down the mountainside.

SOUTHBOUND PASSENGER TRAIN, Nenana River Canyon.

EMPTY COAL TRAIN for Usibelli coal mines, emerging from north portal, Garner tunnel, Nenana River Canyon.

ALL ABOARD

Chapter V

Come, let's trek north on the Alaska Railroad to the present, where the past is alive today, as when it all began, and into the future that is as certain as was the glorious past.

Come to the land of the aurora borealis and the domain of "The Great One", Mount Denali, which embodies the spirit of the land, its people, the Native Americans, and those of us who came later.

Meet those Americans whose ancestors came from another Continent by the land bridge from Siberia to Alaska. See mountains whose basic composition also came from vast distances through the centuries to form what is now the Talkeetna Mountains and the Alaska Range.

Like the many new Alaskans that preceded us in earlier times, our journey begins at the railhead where it all began, Seward.

All Aboard!

SEWARD

Nestled at the head of inspirational Resurrection Bay, Seward is surrounded by mountains, glaciers, and extensive coniferous forests on three sides. Snug inlets, pristine lakes, and scenic bays abound. Close by is the magnificently beautiful Kenai Fjords National Park populated by various species of sea, air and land wildlife living in their natural wilderness state.

At the beginning of steel sit the processing plants and sailing fleet of the thriving fishing industry. Mountains of coal eminating from the Usibelli Coal Mines in Healy sit alongside the Alaska Railroad yards—perpetually being loaded, but never diminishing in size—upon ships bound for Asia. Meanwhile, a short distance away, rail barges are being unloaded for distribution to the whole of interior Alaska.

It is from here that the trek north leads to the kaleidoscope of unparalleled beauty, geological intrigue, and railroad operations so unqiue as to set it distinctively apart from other railways of the world.

SEWARD TO PORTAGE

Wedged in between the glacier covered Kenai Mountains averaging 5000ft/1524m in height, the Alaska Railroad turns its back on Resurrection Bay and heads almost due north. Initially the ascending grade is not severe, but at M.P.-7 the line assumes a 2.2% ruling grade to Divide, M.P.-12. This is the first of three summit crossings challenged by the railroad in its trek north to

Fairbanks. It is reached at a modest, but dramatic, elevation of 700ft/213.3m.

To reach the crest of the first summit the line proceeds, initially, on this moderate ascending grade through a dense forest of coastal conifers. Beyond timberline, in the highlands, is the realm of wild goats. Resurrection River, M.P.-3, is crossed at two isolated points. Below are the frigid, silt loaded waters coming down from the massive Harding Glacier located in the Kenai Fjord National Park. At M.P.-6, Salmon Creek is crossed as the line enters Chugach National Forest, 5,940,000 acres/2,404,000 hectares. The low point of this forest is sea level, the high point is 13,176ft/4005m. Bear Lake, M.P.-6.5, to the east, is passed as the line penetrates this glorious wilderness of wild animals, wild rivers, emerald green lakes, and uncertain weather. The throbbing of diesel-electric locomotives has increased with ferocity as the climb stiffens to become muffled later at M.P.-11.3, as the train penetrates a unique, snowshed/tunnel/snowshed complex. The initial snowshed is 225ft/68.5m long, the adjoining tunnel 113ft/24.4m long, and the north snowshed 460ft/140m long.

Bursting out of this complex, Divide M.P.-12, is reached, and the first summit has been conquered. The line is now on a mountainous shelf in preparation for the descent on a 2.4% grade to the Snow River crossing. To the east rises one of the many panoramas of matchless scenic gems along the line. Far below, the Snow River and South Fork River embrace Paradise Peak, 6182ft/1884m, as they converge to form the main channel of the Snow River. Both north and south of this peak, glaciated mountains of equal grandeur dominate this panorama. With a sharp eye, and good weather, one might see the residents of the domain—bear, moose, and waterfowl.

Snow River, as seen from the summit at Divide, is traversed at M.P.-14.5. The crossing takes place over a four unit thru truss bridge, 600ft/182.8m long, located on an "S" shaped curve. The railroad is now located at the base of Sheep Mountain, 4780ft/1457.3m high. From M.P.-18 to M.P.-23.5, Lawing, the line follows the shore of treacherous Kenai Lake. It is a very large body of water, "S" shaped in configuration situated west of the railroad.

As with so many of Alaska's large lakes, boating is at a minimum. The water is very cold and the lake is plagued by sudden, unannounced, strong winds. This causes water turbulance and waves of a magnitude and ferocity of the high seas. Any dunking that might occur as a result of this upheaval, can and does cause hypothermia, and ultimately, if submerged, death!

EAGLE

39

From Crown Point, M.P.-24.5, the line hugs the shore of Lower and Middle Trail Lakes, to the east. At Moose Pass, M.P.-29.5, a wooden trestle 285ft/86.8m long is crossed. To the west is contiguous Upper Trail Lake. The railroad parallels it until M.P.-33. Here it crosses a confluence of Trail River and Johnson Creek over a wooden trestle 375ft/114.3m long. All along this pristine lake system snow and glacier covered mountains, populated by the beautiful white dall sheep, rise straight up from the shores. Moose Pass, a little village tucked in at the base of this network of lakes, glaciers and mountains, acts as a distribution point for railroad freight to the rest of the Kenai Peninsula and Cool Inlet oil fields. The total scene could only be described in the words of a poet and by the brush of an artist inspired by celestial direction.

From M.P.-33 to Grandview, M.P.-45, the line assumes a climb of 2%. It proceeds in an easterly direction to cross the second summit, Grandview, at an altitude of 1063ft/324m.

Perched on a mountain ledge the railroad skirts a panorama, to the east, of unequivocal and mesmerizing beauty. It is the valley of the Trail River, the hanging Trail Glacier, and the adjoining ice fields of massive proportions fading off into the horizon. Winter snows reach levels of 20ft/6m to 30ft/9m. Because of this extensive snow fall, the railroad in this region is confronted with snow and ice, and rock slides. Grandview is also an end-point for numerous winter ski trips from Anchorage provided by the railroad.

From this point, it's a steady descent to Portage, at sea level, situated on the shores of Turnagain Arm. At M.P.-47.5 the grade assumes a descent of 3%. Passing through this overwhelming region one feels insignificant in comparison to its magnitude and beauty. At M.P.-47.2 the line crosses a 60ft/18.2m deck girder bridge. Slowly the railroad turns to the east on its 3% descent to encounter directly in its path, Bartlet Glacier! Shortly after sighting this ice mass, the line makes a very sharp hair-pin turn on itself. This turn occurs 300ft/91.4m in front of the face of the glacier. A reversed curve to the north puts the railroad in direct line with another potentially formidable obstruction. With Deadman Glacier looking down on this whole scene from the mountains to the east, the railroad crosses over Placier River on a deck truss bridge 133ft/40m long. Immediately it plunges into the first of a series of five tunnels separated at two points by small bridges. This engineering feat rests on a shoulder of glacier scarred and glacier covered Beverly Peak, 5575ft/1699m high. Far below, to the east of the railroad is the angry Placier River, continuously eroding the base of this very narrow canyon as it gouges its way down to Turnagain Arm. Recently the five tunnels have been enlarged to accommodate larger and greater freight movements. The fifth tunnel of the original six tunnel

concept has been day-lighted in concert with the current modernization program. It is in this region, up until 1951, that the railroad descended by a series of loops built on wooden trestles, and covered in some places by snowsheds. The receding Bartlett Glacier allowed the present arrangement, but at the cost of a 3% grade. This is the steepest grade on the main line. Some of the timbers of this earlier operation can still be seen here.

Passing through the last tunnel the line makes a broad "S" shaped curve. To the east is Spencer Glacier. Placier River, again, is crossed at M.P.-54.1 over a 200ft/60.9m thru truss bridge. From here it is directly north on a gradually descending course to Portage, M.P.-64. To the west is the extensive braided system of the Placier River. To the east is a magnificent wall of scarred and jagged glaciered mountains, separated periodically by "U" shaped glacier derived valleys. Skookum Glacier dips down like a white mantle from Carpathian Peak, at 4000ft/1219m in height. It is an extension of an extensive ice field that trails down, eastward, to the shores of the Gulf of Alaska.

Emerging from the shadow of these mountains, the railroad enters the flatlands at Portage. To the east is world famous Portage Glacier, with Portage Lake sitting at its base, filled with blue tinted icebergs. A siding is passed at M.P.-63 which houses in the winter the snow fleet ready to fight winter's insults. Finally, at M.P.-64 the railroad is in Portage. This is the junction point with the other main-line from Whittier, 12mi/20km, to the east. It was in Portage, during the 1964 earthquake which measured 8.4 on the Richter Scale, that the land sank 10 to 12 feet/3 to 3.65m. The sea engulfed this sunken region with a resulting total devastation of the ground cover. Dead trees, to this day, stand as monuments to the lethal effects of this calamity. An exceptionally beautiful station and many homes were so completely destroyed that there is very little trace of any remnants. Surrounding the immediate area on three sides, are the ever present Chugach and Kenai Mountains. Since these mountains rise directly out of the sea to exhibit their bald, ice age profile, one gets an illusion of far greater vertical magnitude than what actually exists. Their average elevation is approximately 4500ft/1371m. Although the Alaskan Railroad is primarily a north/south line, it is here that it turns westward for 50mi/83.3km to reach Anchorage. Leaving Portage, the railroad crosses Twenty Mile River on an impressive deck truss bridge, 490ft/149.3m long. In the distance to the north is Twenty Mile Glacier. Pressed up against the face of the mountains, the railroad reenters the Chugach National Forest and proceeds somewhat inland from the waters of Turnagain Arm. Because of this close proximity to the mountains, many sections along the line have been designated as slide zones. M.P.-74.5 brings the line into

Girdwood, the home of Alaska's famous ski resort, Alyeska. Hopefully, this will be the site of a future Winter Olympics.

Leaving Girdwood over a sharp curve to the south and then to the west, the line assumes its true character. It appears to be heading out into the cold waters of Turnagain Arm; and, to some degree it does. Riding above sea level at approximatley 40ft/12m, much of the line has been rebuilt after the earthquake on causeways situated away from the mountains. While avoiding periodic snow and rock avalanches, the line must, twice daily, face a massive onslaught of water coming in from Cook Inlet. Tides in the spring have a maximum daily range of 38.9ft/11.9m. This is one of the highest tides in the world, second only to those in the Bay of Fundy in Nova Scotia, Canada. Since the rise and fall can be very large in shallow, narrow fjords such as Turnagain Arm, the incoming tide can move in as a "bore"; i.e., a solid wall of water moving as one mass to a height, at times, of 6ft/1.8m. Thus, this body of water is unsafe for small boats, and for humans who may venture out onto the adjoining mud flats at low tide. The extensive railroad causeway feels the brunt of the onslaught.

Williwaws, or sudden violent winds, can and do raise havoc with the railroad. These are found in areas of large bodies of inland water, such as lakes and coastal fjords, especially in the vicinity of glaciers. Turnagain Arm has all the ingredients for the development of this phenomenon. Years ago on the line into Whittier, these winds blew several freight cars right off the main line. As the train left the east portal of Portage tunnel and proceeded on to an adjoining wooden trestle, Williwaws came down Bear Valley from the surrounding glaciers to topple this consist.

Crossing numerous small bridges and culverts, the line makes its serpentine trek to Anchorage. Since Girdwood, the line has been on the edge of Chugach State Park's 490,000 acres/198,000 hectares. In the distant west the Chigmit Mountains, with a string of volcanoes, looms into view. Dominant at first glance is Mt. Spurr, 11,000ft/3353.8m. This mountain, as well as its sister peaks, (as is usually the case with Alaskan mountains) springs directly out of the water. When the setting sun illuminates this perpetual cover of white which rests on a base of icy blue water, a blaze of fiery red lights up the mountains, creating a syncopating harmony of brilliant hues.

Potter, M.P.-101, is the point of departure of the railroad from its flirtation with the sea. Gradually, decreasing forests are replaced with the increasing monotony of urbanization. One more brief encounter with the sea occurs as the line passes across Bootlegger Cove on a causeway and enters Anchorage, M.P.-114.

While Juneau is the legislative capital of Alaska, Anchorage cradled between the mountains and the sea, is the cultural, economic, and transportation hub. A city of 250,000 residents, it has approximately one-half of the state's population. The administrative headquarters and dispatch point for the entire railroad are located here. Extensive shops house most of the railroad's locomotives and contain facilities for the maintenance of its rolling stock.

Although Anchorage possesses a dock for ocean going vessels, its operation can best be described as modest. Cook Inlet tides with their great fluctuations act as a detriment, limiting its true potential. Situated in the shadows of the marshalling yards of the railroad, the dock receives virtually all of Sea-Land's containers destined for interior Alaska.

Anchorage's greater prominence on the transportation scene, however, is the role it plays in the airline industry. Beside serving as a stop for numerous intracontinental flights, it serves as an intermediate terminal for virtually all airlines of American, European, and Asian origin, during their transpolar flights.

ANCHORAGE TO TALKEETNA

As one leaves Anchorage, M.P.-114.3, the relative abruptness of transition into a wilderness region, so common in Alaska, is not evident. It is not until Eklutna, M.P.-142.2, that one senses a return to Alaska's vast remoteness. Complexes of business and industry initially prevail along the right-of-way. These gradually give way to clusters of homes that become increasingly scattered as the line travels north.

While the prevailing grade north to Curry, M.P.-248.5, is an ascent of 1%, the initial mileage out of Anchorage is a descent. A low point of 35ft/10.6m above sea level is reached at M.P.-142.8 just prior to the crossing of the great delta of the Knik and Matanuska Rivers. Before reaching this point, periodic views of Knik Arm can be seen to the west. A short distance beyond the town of Eagle River, M.P.-127.5, a deck girder bridge spanning a river of the same name, is crossed. It is 308ft/93.8m long. Upon reaching Eklutna, M.P.-142.3, there is a dramatic change in the whole scene. As one passes through this village, vestiges of the past dominate the scene. A national historic landmark, St. Nicholas Russian Orthodox Church, and a unique Indian Cemetery, are located here. The graves are covered by little white houses distinctively identified by their unique Russian crosses. From this point the railroad appears to be heading straight for the mountains. What has happened is that Knik Arm with its adjoining low lands, and the rugged Chugach Mountains have converged. The broad lowlands before Eklutna have now become a narrow shelf before finally giving way to the Knik and Matanuska River crossing. The railroad, prior to the river crossing, is tucked into the base of the virtually vertical walls of the massive Chugach Mountains. This short portion of the line from M.P.-142.5 to M.P.-146.4 is,

for obvious reasons, designated a slide zone. From an aesthetic perspective, and description demands superlatives. Since the line is almost at sea level, and the mountains reach an altitude of 7000ft/2134m, the enormity of this vertical relief is awesome.

Just as quickly as the railroad skirts the mountains, it abruptly turns away from them to cross the broad delta of the Knik and Matanuska Rivers. Knik River is crossed on a combination thru-truss and girder bridge, 864ft/263m long, at M.P.-146.5. To cross the Matanuska River, isolated truss bridges in a series from M.P.-147 to M.P.-149 are traversed. From this point to Talkeetna and beyond, the railroad passes through a divergent topography. We are coming into an area of pastoral farms and what appear to be endless forests and lakes. This region of spruce, birch, and aspen trees is criss-crossed by a multitude of fish-laden streams, rivers and lakes.

What one notices, as these initial flat lands are crossed at the Matanuska and Knik Rivers, is that they seem to blend into the sea of the shallow Knik Arm. When one understands the geological formation of these flats, it will be easy to see how these "milky" rivers will one day "push back", further, the waters of Knik Arm.

These lowlands are bordered on the east by the Talkeetna Mountains, and on the north and west by the Alaska Range. Originally this region was floored with sedimentary rocks, and was subsequently inundated by extensive glaciers coming down from the surrounding mountains. This resulting topography is in part derived from the erosive actions of these glaciers, and partly from the deposition of moraine and gravel. The lowlands became filled with sand, gravel and rock. Vegetation grew and died in a cyclic manner to form organic accumulation, peat, and subsequently coal. The latter is found in the Matanuska Valley, which in the past was an active coal mining region. The activity has declined, but hopefully will be reactivated soon.

As the glaciers retreated they left behind these lakes. The erosive effect of the rivers and glaciers still continues. The resulting sediment is very fine, and this imparts a "milky" appearance to the Knik and Matanuska rivers. Thus, looking out to Knik Arm at low tide, one sees extensive mud flats as testimonial of an earlier and present filling effect from this continued deposition—a fine example of living geological evolution is witnessed.

Continuing north, with luck, moose may be seen on these flats. Matanuska Junction is reached at M.P.-151. Here begins the 7mi/11.6km branch to Palmer. Originally it extended further to the coal mines at Jonesville and Eska and the projected mines at Chickaloon. Although track beyond Palmer has been removed, it is hoped that with a resurgence of the mines, coal will be trucked to Palmer and then shifted to rail transport at this point. Presently the railroad line hauls extensive gravel from

here to Anchorage.

This valley, and that along the mainline to Wasilla comprise the great dairy and vegetable farming center of Alaska. These regions were originally settled by farmers from Minnesota, Wisconsin, and Michigan. Its appearance somehwat resembles pastoral Vermont. Wasilla, M.P.-159.8, a fast growing community, is in fact not only an extension of the suburbia of Anchorage, but also a service area for sportsmen, farmers, and miners. Beyond is a wilderness region of lakes, forests, rivers, and isolated hamlets. Hugging the Susitna River, the railroad continues in almost a straight line due north. Periodic excellent views of Mt. Denali are to be seen. It is in this region that the winter moose kills by the trains reach massive proportions. With snowfalls up to 15ft/4.6km, moose are forced down to lower levels because snow covers their normal feeding areas. When the right-of-way is cleared of snow, it not only provides an easier route for travel, but also uncovers vegetation for the moose diet. With the numerous curves along the line, the moose remain out of view of the train, until it is upon them. As a result moose become statistics.

Passing through romantically named locations, such as Kashwitna, Goose Creek, Sunshine, and Fish Lake and over countless trestles and bridges, the Alaska Range looms ever greater in the distance. After traveling for 3 hours and 40 minutes, and 112.4mi/187.3km, Talkeetna, M.P.-226.7, is reached.

TALKEETNA

Talkeetna, M.P.-226.7, is a small community located, as its Indian origin describes, at the "meeting of the rivers", the Chulitna, Susitna, and Talkeetna. It is also the start of our photographic essay. Originally it served as a base for gold mining and fur trapping. Now it acts as an embarcation center for an extensive number of world-wide climbers whose goal is to master the great Mount Denali. (Map)

Served by a garage-sized railroad station, the community appears frozen in time. Scattered about almost indiscriminately, the town has an air of the past. Down by the station, passengers greater in number than one might expect, wait both summer and winter for the trains that will take them to their homesteads and adventure in the wilderness north of Talkeetna. The scene is reminiscent of the days when everything from the loaf of bread on the table to the nails holding the house together all came by rail. Household appliances, tools, rough building materials, machinery of all kinds, and food stuffs fill the baggage compartment. Fishermen and hikers swell the entourage, dreaming of the ecstasies that are before them. Many carry rifles, knives, and backpacks, as they prepare to go into the "bush". It is wise that these precautions are taken; when the fishing is good, the "welcoming committee" is usually out in force: black bears! For the next 60 miles the only physical way out is the railroad. It is for this reason that the rail service is continued in the winter, for it is the lifeline to the "outside".

With a couple of blasts on the air horn the train slowly starts off, passing over the Talkeetna River by crossing a double-thru truss bridge, 400ft/121.9m long. Lush green country consisting of thick underbrush, fireweed, and strands of spruce, cottonwood, and birch trees pass in succession. To the immediate west we glide along the silty Susitna River. The silt represents fine grains of sand formed by glacial erosion taking place all along the head waters; however, the majority of streams and rivers that the train continually crosses are clear. These are the fishing holes.

Immediately east of the railroad, and gradually closing in on the line as one heads north, are the Talkeetna Mountains. They range in height from 5000ft/1523.9m to 7000ft/2134m. The peaks and ridges are jagged and rise from deep trough-like valleys. As one continues north, these razor-sharp peaks become flat, rounded, and not so high. This transition is the result of glacial action during the time of the pleistocene ice sheets. The lower ridges were completely over-ridden, and were not subjected to the stresses affecting the higher ridges that rose above the ice level. It was during this period, when the glaciers were formed, that the average atmospheric temperature decreased and the level of the ocean dropped, exposing the land bridge between Siberia and Alaska.

Curry, M.P.-248.5, only a name on the map now, but once an important railroad point, is passed. At one time, a hotel here served the public as an overnight stop during the original three-day trip from Seward to Fairbanks. The grade increases from 1% to 1.75% at this point, maintaining, basically, this stance until Summit, located at Broad Pass. The line passes over the great Susitna River at Gold Creek, M.P.-257.7, on a thru truss bridge, 504ft/153.6m long. It then turns sharply to the east and then to the west in sequence, ever climbing on the way to Summit while it follows the clear waters of the Indian River. Suddenly the train swings into direct line with the great 4558ft/1389.6m monolith, Indian Mountain. One is now in the Denali State Park. A sharp turn to the north, and a crossing of the Indian River over a small truss bridge, brings us to Chulitna, M.P.-273.8, for the final push up hill. Straining hard on the drawbar, our train continues to climb the 1.75% incline to Summit. Gradually emerging from the shadow of Indian Mountain, it passes Chulitna, M.P.-273.8, Chulitina Pass, the nearby lakes, and enters a relatively open landscape.

The route now becomes more tortuous, and with it comes an increasing tempo best described as a concert of harmony in power which eminates from the head end

diesel-electric units. Suddenly, almost like a mirage, the massive and overwhelming Mt. Denali, 20,320ft/6194m appears. Nothing in the immediate vicinity comes close to the height and mass of this mountain. While seeming close to the observer because of its total dominance of the scene, it is in fact 45mi/75km away. Rising directly from a plateau of only 2000ft/609.7m, it realizes its great height within 10mi/17km of the mountain-plain junction. Not only is it the tallest mountain in North America, but it has the distinction of having the greatest vertical relief, 15,000ft/4573m, of any mountain in the world.

This whole region consists of a series of jagged peaks, inhospitable and barren. Rock falls, avalanches, and storms are common. Super-imposed on this framework is a continuous network of extensive glaciers and continuous fresh snow. Consequently, "U" shaped glacier valleys as much as 5mi/9km wide have been formed, flowing over cliffs as high as 3mi/5km. These glaciers are present on both the southern and northern slopes. South facing glaciers however, are larger because of the greater snowfall. Ruth, Tolositna, and Kahiltna glaciers are 40mi/66km to 50mi/83km long and descend to an altitude of 1000ft/304.8m. So it continues for the next 82mi/136km as we travel along a convergent route beside this magnificent 600mi/1000km range until we ultimately pierce it at Windy.

The climb continues, but tapers off to a 0.5%-1.0% grade. Hurricane section house is passed at M.P.-281. At M.P.-284 the train slows down to 5mph/8kph, makes a slight turn to the west, and crosses the famous Hurricane Gulch arched, deck bridge. It measures 918ft/279.8m long and 296ft/91m above the canyon floor. For the next 2mi/3.3km the train passes along a forested ledge high above the Chulitna River. At M.P.-286 the line turns eastward and descends to the approaches of a dramatic horseshoe curve on a 1% grade. Just ahead are the beautiful arrow shaped peaks of the Talkeetna Mountains. Before completing the turn, a 150ft/46m thru-truss bridge is traversed as it crosses Honolulu Creek. It takes 2mi/3.3km to complete this loop. The line turns northward, once again, to pass Alaska's Honolulu, which is but a name on a passing siding, in the middle of nowhere, in this great wilderness region.

Crossing the East Fork of the Chulitina River, M.P.-292.3, over a 140ft/43m deck girder bridge, the line meanders up past Broad Pass, at M.P.-304.3, passing through the thinning boreal forest, a plateau of unique and overwhelming beauty unfolds. Measuring from 5mi/8.3km to 10mi/16.6km in width, and approximately 15mi/24.9km in length, a transitional botanical and biological zone takes us from the forest to this new dimension, the Tiaga/Tundra ecotone. At M.P.-312.5, located at 63 degrees 20 minutes N. Latitude, Summit is crossed. It is located at an altitude of 2360ft/719.5m, and it is the high-

est point on the Alaska Railroad; however, it is the lowest crossing of any railroad in the Rocky Mountain chain. This is the dividing point of the Pacific and Bering Sea watersheds. While summits of mountain ranges generate thoughts of deep crevasses, high bridges and steep grades, the contrary is here the reality.

Wedged in between the Alaska Range and the Talkeetna Mountains in this relatively flat region whose geological origin, in the midst of all these mountains, remains obscure. Here is an Arctic panorama which epitomizes the character of the great northland. It is the land of the tiaga, tundra and the caribou. We are now in a new topographical and ecological dimension. This is Broad Pass. It can capture the mind and soul to such a degree that, as railroad legend has it, upon death one of the retired employees requested his ashes be spread across this land. And, so it was done!

Winter brings on a panorama that presents the classical stereotype of an Alaskan scene. Chill winds and blowing snows conjure up an image of an Eskimo with his dog team mushing across the tundra. At this location, this reality is rather remote, but, the Eskimo may still be there. Instead of holding the reins of a dog team, his hand may very well be the one that guides a throbbing 6,000 HP multi-unit locomotive across the vast arctic interior. Snow drift after snow drift is hurled to the side and to the rear by the permanently fixed front-end snow plow. All the while the engineer's hand hangs heavy on the wailing air horn, for the ever-present moose on the right-of-way is no match for the modern day iron horse.

With cold winter nights, -40F/-40C, comes a spectacular dance in the heavens that makes the heart beat even faster. Like a true kaleidoscope, changing, multicolored streaks of light, accentuated by bright twinkling stars, slither high above the moonlit tundra. This is the land of the Aurora-Borealis, the Northern Lights.

Eskimo legend has it that the aurora is caused by the spirits of the honored deceased—such as a hunter lost during a hunting expedition. These spirits are now playing ball, using the head of a walrus. The successive ever-changing movements of the lights across the sky represent the evidence of the struggle between the spirits in their game.

The scientific explanation is a bit different. It is believed that the molecules, of which the atmosphere is composed, are being struck by charged particles, electrons and protons, eminating from the sun. The earth's magnetic field directs these particles to the polar regions, where they enter the atmosphere, striking the molecules of the atmosphere, and causing them to glow. Personally, I prefer the former explanation.

The tiaga and tundra, which the railroad now traverses, represent a new botanical dimension. Dotting the expanse are small clusters of spruce trees, short and thin in

NORTHBOUND RDC loading passengers and baggage, Talkeetna; M.P.-227.

ED BRUMMOND, engineer, RDC at Talkeetna.

"MAYOR" OF SHERMAN, Alaska—and its only resident—reading the National Geographic magazine while waiting for the train in Talkeetna.

LOADING an infinite variety of baggage into an RDC, Talkeetna.

AMERICAN INDIAN LAD waiting anxiously for the arrival of the passenger train that will take him further into the "bush." Location, Talkeetna.

THE TRAIN WILL STOP anywhere along the line in the "bush" to serve the passengers. Location, Indian Canyon; M.P.-268.4.

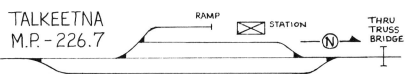

TALKEETNA
M.P. - 226.7

RAMP   ⊠ STATION   —(N)►   THRU TRUSS BRIDGE

NORTHBOUND RDC approaching Indian Mountain, in Indian River Canyon; M.P.-269.6.

CURRY M.P. - 248.5

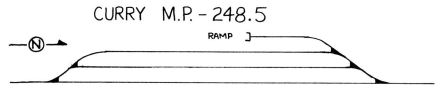

RAMP

46

—N→

GOLD CREEK M.P. - 263.2

SECTION HOUSE ☒

SUSITNA RIVER

THRU TRUSS BRIDGE

RAILROAD CREW celebrating the marriage of the daughter of the Gold Creek, M.P.-263.2, section foreman. Location of train is at Hurricane; M.P.-281.4.

47

SOUTHBOUND RDC. North face of Indian Mountain. Talkeetna range in the background.

—Ⓝ→

CHULITNA M.P. – 273.8

NORTHBOUND FREIGHT train climbing the hill out of Chulitna.

BUSH PASSENGERS waiting for RDC at Hurricane, M.P.-281.4 while express passenger train passes by.

stature, interlaced with numerous lakes. While suggesting a flat alpine terrain, it is best described by a word from the Russian language, tiaga, or "the land of little sticks." The primary blanket cover, however, is tundra, a wet cushion of flowers, berries, and low bushes. Both of these areas are interwoven. From a distance one may perceive that this represents an easy avenue for hiking ventures. It is not!

The tundra is both dry and wet. The former, or alpine tundra has a thin layer of soil, usually over a rocky base, supporting plant life which does not usually grow more than several inches in height. This includes lichen, berry plants, and wild flowers. Wet tundra is usually superimposed on permafrost which means that the soil has a high water content and is permanently frozen. Growing to a relatively uniform height, are dwarfed willows, horsetails, sedges and grasses. Run-off water from snow and rains become sequestered in small pools, due to the permafrost, rather than percolating into the soil. As a result, one has a large grassy quagmire, not to mention a great breeding place for mosquitos and black flies.

Upon this foundation the railroad was built. Surface physical obstacles have been overcome, but the underlying permafrost has not. When you have a mean temperature of 27 degrees F/-3 degrees C, and a soil with a high water content, the sub-strata become frozen. Any peeling back of the soggy tundra (which acts as a source of insulation from the sun's heat in the undisturbed natural state) exposes the underlying strata to atmospheric temperatures and summer melting. This results in a periodic sagging of the roadbed which causes "horizontal curves". As a result, shimming of the rails, and total roadbed re-alignment are a continuous and major ordeal for the railroad.

Once the divide is crossed at Summit M.P.-312.5, the grade starts a 1% descent to Cantwell. The train hugs the west shore of Summit lake, crosses a strip of tiaga, to once again parallel one of the many pristine shallow lakes located in the pass. To the east, up through the valley of the Nenana River, one can see Mt. Deborah, glacier crowned, at 12,339ft/3761.8m, and Mt. Hess at 11,940ft/3640m. It is this east-west valley that separates the Alaska Range from the Talkeetna Mountains.

Magnificent panoramic scenes unfold in every direction as the train gradually descends into Cantwell, M.P.-315.5, after crossing Cantwell Creek on a small girder bridge located asthetically on a reverse curve. At one time, this

HURRICANE M.P. – 281.4

 —Ⓝ→

 SECTION HOUSE

SOUTHBOUND RDC passing over Hurricane Gulch bridge. Alaska range in the background.

NORTHBOUND PASSENGER TRAIN passing over Hurricane Gulch bridge.

small community served as an experimental reindeer station. In addition to containing a small Indian population, it now serves highway travelers as a rest stop and as an intermediate station for highway maintenance.

Leaving Cantwell over a series of reversed curves, the train passes the Reindeer Hills, crosses Windy Creek, and enters Denali National Park. Straight ahead is strikingly awesome Mt. Panorama. Multi-peaked, jagged and treeless, at 6000ft/1829m, this mountain is a representative of the geological origins of this area, 180 million years distant. Originating from basaltic lava flows, the hallmark of this group of mountains is the green stones which impart a dark-green or dark-brown color to their slopes.

What makes this mountain and others along the immediate route appear so high is that one is looking almost directly into a vertical relief of 4000ft/1219m. Clinging precipitously to these jagged walls, the railroad joins the Nenana River at Windy, to pierce the Alaska Range through a slit-like trench. Between Carlo, M.P.-334, the home of a section crew, and M.P.-336 looking south, one can only stare in awe at the strikingly beautiful panoply of mountains. Straddling both sides of the Nenana River, in a 180 degree arc, they appear to gently embrace the whole setting, even though their abrupt vertical rise gives an appearance of fractured, fault-block origin.

In the winter, this is the location of many ice formations.

HURRICANE
GULCH
BRIDGE

M.P. - 284.2

51

SOUTHBOUND FREIGHT on "Horseshoe curve" at Honolulu; M.P.-288.7.
Talkeetna mountains in the background.

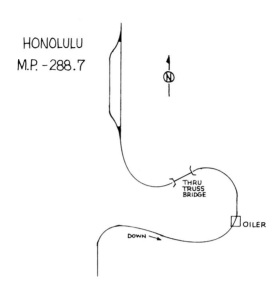

HONOLULU
M.P. -288.7

THRU TRUSS BRIDGE

OILER

DOWN

SOUTHBOUND FREIGHT on south leg of "Horseshoe curve," ascending out of Honolulu.

Although this same problem exists along many sections of the line, it is here, in juxtaposition with the embracing mountains, that one sees the most striking effect. This is new ice, not the old ice from centuries old glaciers coming down from the mountains. It is caused by sequential freezing of the many small streams which pass under the line. Winter's cold temperatures obstruct the flow of water by forming ice on the surface layers. This results in an increase in hydrostatic pressure, which is caused by the everflowing streams. Finally the ice is cracked and underlying water escapes to re-flood this same area. Subsequently, this water is frozen into a new layer of ice. This process continues until, if allowed, it engulfs and covers the track and roadbed.

To counteract this ice formation, holes are cut into the ice near the culverts. Fifty gallon, open ended drums are then inserted into these excavations, followed by the addition of charcoal. The charcoal is ignited and the resulting heat melts the surrounding ice. A flow of water through the culvert is thus initiated. To keep this flow

going in the sub-freezing atmospheric temperatures, salt is added which results in a lower freezing point. In addition, to facilitate this flow, electrical filaments are inserted into the culverts and some of the drums. Electric current from portable generators is then passed through these units to produce heat which melts the ice, and in turn enhances the flow of water. In areas of extreme ice build-up, the mass is bull-dozed out and relocated, by a crane, to the down shoulder of the track. Since it rarely rises above the freezing point during winter in this region, this endless battle continues until spring.

A sinuous course continues northward, all the while hugging the west bank of the Nenana River. Although the descent of the railroad is gradual, the river's flow increases in tempo and ferocity, assuming a steeper degree of descent. Soon the railroad traverses a ledge high above the swirling, cascading white water below. Moose are frequent visitors along the flats of the river as well as along the right-of-way. Further north, along the vertical cliffs of the Nenana River Canyon, the exquisite dahl

sheep are very evident to the naked eye. With luck, almost any kind of bird or animal may be seen, for we are riding along the edge of one of the world's greatest wildlife parks.

At M.P.-342.7 is Oliver. This is a siding that is used in the summer as a meeting point for the north and south-bound passenger trains. While most of the other locations along the Alaska Railroad have Indian names, this one is named after a former employee of the engineering department. Rounding a small lake at M.P.-344, one sees (looking to the east) the Pyramids at 5500ft/1676.8m. Sitting virtually by themselves in the Yanert Valley, they appear much taller than what they actually are. Aptly named, their geometrical symmetry could suggest an Egyptian origin.

Coming into Denali Park Station, M.P.-347.7, the Alaska Railroad crosses the spectacular Riley Creek trestle. This deck girder bridge is 570ft/173.7m long, and is the second-highest on the system. Below is the confluence of the Riley and Hines creeks. Although we are a

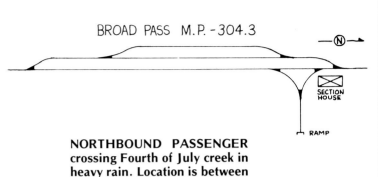

BROAD PASS M.P. -304.3

SECTION HOUSE

RAMP

NORTHBOUND PASSENGER crossing Fourth of July creek in heavy rain. Location is between Colorado and Broad Pass.

matter of yards from the Denali Park station, the primevil wilderness prevails. It would not be surprising to see a bear or a moose step out into full view at any time. This is the door step of "the great one".

Denali National Park

Denali National Park is one of the world's greatest wilderness areas. Established in 1917, and enlarged in 1980, this region of 6 million acres/2.43million hectares, is about one third the size of Switzerland. Adjacent to this region, at its southeast boundary, is Denali State Park. This adds an additional 324,240 acres/131,218 hectares to this primeval expanse. Located at approximately 63 degrees north parallel, which is 200mi/333.3km south of the arctic circle, it is entirely within the subarctic climatic zone.

It is not only with respect to latitude that this habitat claims its distinction, but also literally from the heavens. Mt. Denali, "The Great One" at 20,320ft/6194m, like a mythical god of the north, dominates the scene. Standing close by is Mt. Menale (Foraker), at 17,395ft/5303.3m. According to Indian lore, this mountain is also known as "Denali's wife." Between them they send out, on their southern slopes, an extensive glacial cover reaching to the extremely low altitude of 1000ft/304.8m. Cradled in this blanket of ice and snow stand Mt. Hunter, 14,580ft/4445m, Mt. Silvertone, 13,220ft/4030.4m, and many other peaks over 10,000ft/3048.7m. Yet, singularly, nothing could be more awesome than the Kichatna Mountains. Situated at the southwest corner of the park, the Cathedral

spires within this group represent the prototype which inspires artists to create mountain images.

Encompassed within this glaciated jagged land lies a boreal forest interwoven with tiaga and tundra. One-hundred and fifty-five species of birds, and thirty-seven varieties of mammals inhabit this representative of the "bitter north." Birds arrive here from many distant regions and continents to supplement the native birds such as the great horned owl, the ptarmigan and the sacred bird of the Indians, the raven. Perhaps one of the most significant features of this area is that one quickly realizes that man is the intruder. Even the aboriginal Athabaskans only passed through on their hunts. For then, as today, there are no established communities in this region. The 575,000 yearly visitors just pass through on their hunt for the freedom of the wilderness. Fortunately they are armed only with cameras.

For most visitors this excursion is limited to the 89mi/148km of road to Wonder Lake, using park service shuttle buses. Backpackers, however, with some restrictions, have the whole park in which to tramp about. And, what a trek this can be. From a low of 525ft/160m to a high point of 20,320ft/6194m, one can study and enjoy the living world and its origins. In early summer, 450 species of wild flowers and plant life fill this region. From the small yellow-cheeked vole, to the 1600lb/727kg moose, the region is the domain of many species of northern wildlife. Arctic hare, lynx, fox, wolves, caribou, bear, and wolverine are notable examples. At higher altitudes, the beautiful dahl sheep grace the slopes of the steep mountains.

Many may have visited this wilderness region but none can ever say that they have ever totally seen it!

Denali National Park to Healy

Boarding the train at Denali Park station for the trip to Fairbanks, one can see the distant saw-toothed peaks of the Alaska Range. They loom above a broad valley to the east, to form a stupendous mountain well. This is the Mt. Hayes group, 13,470ft/4106.7m, situated just outside of the national park.

Between Denali Park Station, M.P.-348, and Healy M.P.-358, lies one of the silent beauties in the area. If Mt. Denali is one of the most sought after scenic displays Nenana River Canyon is one of the jewels most often missed by the average visitor. Approximately one-half of it is located in the park, the other half should be, for it's a geological dream.

The railroad passes along a shoulder of Mt. Healy all the way to Healy. Its route is so precarious that passenger trains are limited to 20mph/33kmph. Initially, the route is lush green, but gradually the line assumes a sinuous course through a canyon of multi-colored rock eroded, fractured, and fragmented by earthquakes and geological evolution.

Shortly after leaving the station, the park road is crossed, a small cut is traversed, and suddenly there is an abrupt change in the landscape. The railroad is now on a ledge, hundreds of feet/meters above the Nenana River. Tucked in between the river and the ledge is small, but elegant Horseshoe Lake. Originally it was a hair-pin curve on the Nenana River. Time changed the course of the river leaving this isolated, crystal clear, body of water to the moose and beavers which frequent the region.

At M.P.-350 the railroad takes an abrupt swing around a sharp curve in a northerly direction. The line now sits on the shoulder of a ledge that is crumbling apart. Almost straight down is the tormented Nenana River, a mass of white water. Literally laced together with steel cables attached to sunken metal beams, the roadbed and the mountainside are tenuously held in position. The mountain is moving and so is the railroad. At several locations along the line, as one proceeds up the canyon, the remnants of earlier trackwork can be seen. It rests, illogically, below the mainline.

One-half mile beyond, a deck-truss bridge, 225ft/69m, is crossed. Sitting photogenically high up on the side of the mountain, the passage of a train over this structure, as viewed from the canyon floor, is utterly spectacular. From this vantage point the peak is sharply pointed against the sky, presenting a truly classical mountain railroad setting.

Proceeding cautiously along the line, a 369ft/112.4m spidery truss trestle, at M.P.-351.4, has been placed to bridge a fissure in the side of the mountain. Several smaller bridges are encountered before a combination wooden trestle and deck girder bridge, 186ft/56.6m long, is crossed. Amid this scenic splendor, man adds a new dimension far below in the river; it's the sports enthusiast in his kayak, or rubber raft, matching wits with the fierce current.

Just beyond this location sits the single greatest maintenance problem for the railroad. Turning sharply to the east, one passes over the infamous "million dollar curve", M.P.-353. Actually it is a **multi-million** dollar endeavor. Constant maintenance and rebuilding represent an annual necessity. Still, in spite of all these corrective efforts, the line has been cursed with periodic derailments.

The problem is caused by the constant movement of the mountains due to their sedimentary-permafrost composition. As a whole unit, the roadbed drifts continuously toward the canyon floor. Consequently, new track is continuously being rebuilt over the base of the old track. Wooden piles have been driven into the sub-surface and laced with steel cables in an attempt to maintain the tracks in place. Further, wood cribbing is added at specific locations where the whole railroad ledge is on the verge of disappearing.

A short distance from this site the train enters a curved tunnel 200ft/60.9m long. Piercing the north portal of the Moody tunnel, we enter a new dimension. Wedged in between perpendicular walls, very closely spaced, the Alaska Railroad sits once again on a precarious, unstable, edge. Deep down below, the wretching Nenana River works at changing the continent through constant erosion as it did millions of years ago. The river is considered unsafe for human navigation. If it were not for the extreme structural support given to the roadbed, the railroad line would be unsafe as well. Further down the line, old hopper cars have been pushed into the river in an attempt to hold back the canyon wall. Gradually, they are being covered up by the shifting mountains and the falling debris.

As one travels through the canyon, one journeys into the past as well as the present, seeing the origins of the future. On these walls are written the geological hieroglyphics of the Alaska Range. Fractured sedimentary and metamorphic rock from previous earthquakes, on the west wall of the canyon, tell us something of the recent past. The ledge upon which the railroad was built, however, was deposited millions of years ago when this spot was below sea level. Some contend that the east wall was part of the original ancient North American Continent. Just as the Yukon River today deposits the sediment of the Nenana River in the Bering Sea, so did sediment from various world wide origins become deposited in the shallow seas covering what is today interior Alaska. Increasing pressure and heat changed this sediment into metamorphic rock. While this rock on the ledge dates back one-billion years, that of the Denali Fault is much younger.

Intense pressure along this existing fault, sixty million years ago, caused it to rip open. The land buckled and folded on itself to cause a great uplift of the mass. Earthquakes ensued, accompanied by great volcanic activity. Lava poured over this flatland, and volcanic ash covered and embedded itself in the igneous rock. The Alaska Range was born! While this resulted in the formation of the Alaska Range, the geological climax was yet to come. Deep in the bowels of the earth a chamber of magma cooled slowly, but hardened rapidly. Suddenly, as one great mass, it rose to the surface to an altitude of 20,320ft/6194m. Mt. Denali was born! Much later, a second group of mountains were formed. These are called the Outer Range. Geologically, these rocks are much older than those in the central Alaska Range.

As one passes through a series of deck-truss bridges on the way to Garner, M.P.-355.7, beautiful dahl sheep may be seen on the east wall of the canyon. It is a unique opportunity to see these beautiful animals from so close a vantage point.

After passing the section house at Garner, a timberlined tunnel, approximately 200 ft/60.9m in length, is pierced. At one time, the north end of the tunnel sported a rock shed. Several years ago it was dismantled. The rocks from the imposing mountain face continue to fall, but the trains pass through unscathed.

The whole area is a mass of color. Volcanic ash from the past has tinted the mountains various shades of yellow, orange, white and red. Off in the distance, as we approach Healy, seams of lignite appear in the sandstone bluffs. A few miles down the track we are out of the canyon and have arrived in Healy, M.P.-358.7. At one time, not too long ago, this was an important division point for the railroad. It sported a large station, engine house, and a three-story railroad hotel. Fairbanks and Anchorage crews still change here, but the physical properties are all gone. What remains, however, is increasing coal tonnage coming from the Usibelli Coal Mines. It is, indeed, the largest shipper on the line.

From here it's a "down hill" run to Nenana, M.P.-411.7. The line drops from an elevation of 1400ft/426.8m to approximately 350ft/106.7m. Grade changes vary from a maximum of one-percent descent to stretches of relatively level track at Clear Site, M.P.-392.9. Clear is one of the lowest sections of the Alaska Railroad in the interior. We are now in the zone of discontinuous permafrost. This is clearly evident in that the trees have become visibly smaller, stunted, and in many cases disfigured. In the immediate vicinity of Healy many spruce trees appear gnarled with unilateral, flagged, tree limbs. Incessant winds constantly blowing from a single direction are responsible for this oddity. Wildlife throughout this area, however, is still somewhat abundant. Bear, sheep, moose, wolves and coyotes, with luck, may be seen. Shortly after leaving Healy the Usibelli coal tipple is passed. It is situated to the east of the right-of-way. Presently this region has the only active coal mining area in Alaska. It is from this tipple that coal is loaded into hopper cars, ultimately destined for Korea. Locally, shipments are made north to the Fairbanks area.

Lignite, M.P.-362, is appropriately named for in effect, it truly describes Alaska's coal. As one passes through this region, seams of lignite can seen embedded in the zebra striped sandstone cliffs which parallel the tracks. Anthracite coal which is geologically much older than Alaska's lignite, is not to be found here.

At Ferry, M.P.-371, a double-thru truss bridge 400ft/121.6m, is crossed. It is located on a scenic "S" shaped curve. The railroad is now on the east bank of the Nenana River, and assumes this course all the way to Nenana. On both ends of the bridge tooth-like spikes straddle the rails and roadbed. These are designed to prevent automobiles from using the bridge as a common corridor. Starting at the north end of the bridge, 40mi/66.6km of dirt road leads into an otherwise inaccessible domain. Gold mining and caribou hunting are the primary attractions. To accommodate these people with their multitude of vehicles and all-terrain equipment, the railroad maintains, at Healy, flat car loading facilities for subsequent railroad transport across the bridge. In the winter, the courageous cross the frozen Nenana River by driving their vehicles across the ice! This is fraught with great danger for the river is swift, deep and very cold. While appearing solid, the integrity of the ice, cradled in the current, is always

BROAD PASS northbound freight.

open to question.

Panquinque Creek, M.P.-365, in the winter, is a source of great aggravation. What is usually a placid stream, at this time of year, has glacial formation, which causes an extreme overflow of water that progressively grows into great masses of ice. Resulting pressure is so great that it has been known to raise the bridge right off its pedestals.

An apparent biological devastation appears to have occurred at Rex, M.P.-387, and for some miles northward. Where once stately trees covered the landscape, now environmental insult is evident. Decades old trees remain dwarfed, not due to a genetic aberration or even climatic insult. It is, rather, the result of the underlying permafrost. Roots of many of the trees are so shallow that some can be uprooted with one's bare hands. At Rex is also located a gravel pit which serves the needs of the railroad as a source of track ballast.

What appears so bland in the summer, turns into a riot of color and beauty in the autumn. But it's the winter's crystalline artistry that steals the environmental show—the creation of the unique hoar-frost. Clinging precipitously to the branches of trees, poles, and virtually all physical objects, frozen molecules of atmospheric moisture cover the scene in a kaleidoscopic pattern of white. This formation is based on the physical fact that air at warm temperatures can hold greater amounts of water in suspension, but with subsequent cooling the air loses some of its suspended moisture which then becomes deposited on cold objects throughout the immediate environment.

Continuing northward, Clear Site, M.P.-392.9, a U.S.A.F. military installation, is passed. On southbound trains the grandeur of Mt. Denali may be seen here and at many other points along this particular segment of the line.

Nenana to Fairbanks

Coming into Nenana, M.P.-411, the railroad swings almost 90 degrees to the east to run parallel with the Tanana River. In the winter one can see, to the northwest, tug boats and barges stored along the banks of the Nenana River at its confluence with the Tanana River. In the summer, these same barges are tied up along the south bank of the Tanana River, heavily laden with an infinite variety of goods. Supplies will be ferried down river to the Yukon River throughout the summer, serving all the villages en route, much like it was, as the Indians say, "in the ole days." Although the Nenana Station is now closed, passenger trains, upon request, still stop to service the community. Listen closely, for one can hear many of the locals going hard at it in their native Athabascan tongue.

Nenana is the home of the world famous Nenana River Ice Classic. By guessing the exact month, day, hour, and minute, that the spring ice breakup occurs, one can walk away with as much as $100,000. Wedged in between the Tanana River and the railroad is the "break-up" office; alongside it sits one of the famous tripods. This office records the initial ice flow accurately indicating the actual breakup. In the winter, a similar tripod sits in the middle of the river, connected with timing devices in the Classic office, to record the annual event.

Leaving Nenana, one should sit on the river side of the car. It is from this vantage point that many interesting views can be obtained. As we head down along the Tanana River the train makes another 90 degree turn to proceed in a southerly direction. Straining hard it climbs a 1% grade which will take the train around a 180 degree hairpin curve, placing it in a northward direction once again as it continues to gain altitude. Without impeding river traffic, the great glacier fed Tanana River is traversed by passing over the 700ft/213.3m Mears Memorial truss bridge. It has one of the longest spans of its kind in the world. On the northern end of this bridge, on July 15th, 1923, President Harding drove in the Golden Spike to mark the completion of the Alaska Railroad. Close observation from the bridge, down to the shores of the river, reveals many Indian fish-wheels. They are powered by the current of the river rotating the wheel with a circular movement a full 360 degrees. Attached to the ends are basket-like scoops which trap the migrating salmon as they swim upstream to spawn. Along the shores of the Tanana River drying salmon racks bear testimony to the native fisherman's success.

Winter's transformation of the same area is numbing. The sounds of silt and gravel flowing along with the current of the river are no longer heard. Instead, all is quiet, dead still, except for the whisps of wind that stir up the mantle of snow in a spiral swirl. The region is one great expanse of white. Howling dogs pierce the stillness of the day with their mournful cries, while their masters continuously stoke the much needed wood fires. White plumes of smoke from their homes and cabins dot the landscape. A distant odor of burned wood permeates the community. Although the train whistle is crisp and clear and seemingly close by, it can be many miles away. With sub-zero cold at -40F/-40C, a fog descends upon the community. Although the day may be sunny, the visibility within the village is no clearer than that of a London fog. This condensation, known as ice fog, is a unique phenomenon of the Arctic. Necessary for this formation are sub-zero temperatures, with a clear sky and an absence of wind. As the sun retreats below the horizon, there is a warming of the ground surface. Keep in mind that with a clear sky the earth radiates its heat energy to higher altitudes. This, therefore, cools the ground air. With no wind present, a situation known as inversion exists, whereby the cold stagnant ground air acts as a cover on the earth and the warmer air rises to higher elevations. Concomitant with this phenomenon is the production, and subsequent trapping, of water vapor which is a by-product of our respiratory processes, and other forms of combustion. Since cold air holds less moisture than warm air, the moisture condenses into ice crystals. Trapped in these ice crystals are other potentially toxic pullutants, such as carbon monoxide, nitrogen, and sulfa-oxides which may be present in the air. Thus, ice fog is pretty much limited to the ground surfaces and may be absent above an altitude of 100ft/30.4m. Within a matter of a few feet, a 60 car freight train can be swallowed up within this mantle of white, to disappear from one's eyes, save for the final faint flow of the oscillating light of the caboose.

Bursting out of the ice fog a few miles north of Nenana, one might see an Indian hunter riding alongside the train with his Iron Dog (snow machine). However, the "piece de resistance" is the moment when one sees the Alaskan with his dog team gliding across the tiaga to a destination, the primary goal of which often is nothing more than survival.

We are now truly in the Land of the Midnight Sun as the train continues on to Fairbanks. Generally speaking, north of the Alaska Range the day lengthens during the equinox to 21 hours and 49 minutes of daylight. However, when one considers the effects of the twilight at this time of the year, one can fully appreciate that it is actually daylight for 24 hours. This situation exists from May 15th until July 23rd when the civil twilight never ends because the sun never falls more than 6 degrees below the horizon. At midnight, one can sit back in the passenger coach, and enjoy his favorite magazine or newspaper, without the benefit of any external light source.

As the train continues to change latitudes, in its northern trek, a vast expanse of marshy flat land appears to the west of the train. Hundreds upon hundreds of lakes interlace this area to form a unique watery labyrinth and ecosystem. This is known as the Minto Flats. Fish, birds and animals abound. The United States Fish and Wildlife Service considers this to be "one of the highest quality water fowl nesting habitats on the North American Continent." Beaver, muskrat, moose, ducks, geese, and pike call this area home. Dotted throughout this area are Indian caches tilted crazily upward on stilts, abandoned to the elements, as is the old town of Minto itself.

As one gets closer to Fairbanks, the train passes along the base of the Dunbar Hills. Rising to a height of approximately 150ft/457m, the area is clothed in a heavy growth of birch, aspen, and spruce trees. Particularly in the autumn of the year it looks very much like northern New England. Because of permafrost, the valley vegetation consists of small brush and alpine-like islands of spruce trees. In contrast, the surrounding hills have decreased amounts of permafrost. These ice free areas up

SOUTHBOUND PASSENGER TRAIN along Summit Lake near Summit M.P.-312.5. Thunderstorm approaching.

along the hillsides are covered with a growth of heavy timber, paradoxically at higher altitudes.

Dunbar, M.P.-431.7, is quickly and unceremoniously passed. It is the start of the train to Livengood and Tolovana Gold Mining region, 65mi/108km to the north. Thirty-seven minutes later, at M.P.-456.2, Dome is passed. This is the northernmost point on the railroad.

Shortly after leaving Dome one becomes increasingly aware that automobiles are coming into view. At M.P.-461.4 the local highway system is crossed for the first time. A short distance up the line, Happy, M.P.-463, is passed. It was from here that the 3ft/91.4cm narrow gauge Tanana Valley Railroad appeared to follow a rabbit trail to Fox and Chatanika during the Gold Rush Days. Looking to the west, at the highway crossing, the harbinger of the future economy of the region is seen—extensive greenhouses—in conjunction with increasing agricultural acreage. One is now 7 miles/11.6km from Fairbanks.

Between M.P.-466 and 467 the train passes through the University of Alaska, Fairbanks. Sitting on both sides of the railroad is the Fairbanks Research Farm Agricultural and Forestry Station. A short distance up the track is the contiguous campus of the University of Alaska. Comprising a total area of 2300 acres/1930.7 hectares, this "star of the north" was originally established as an agricultural experimental station on March 22, 1906. This unit became the nidus, and the chief reason, that in 1922 a college was established in this region. In 1935 the name was changed to the University of Alaska. With almost 5000 students pursuing studies in a multitude of endeavors, the university has developed departments of expertise in numerous fields. These include petroleum recovering technology, fundamental tectronics, mineral resource identification, water-air-climate relationships, human issues and the area of specialized education, and renewable resources including agriculture and forestry.

Self-evident is the agricultural research unit. To develop a viable society in the north, one cannot simply apply by rote the conclusions gained from other latitudes and expect the same results. Plants and animals, as well as humans in interior Alaska, are subject to day lengths or photo periods, and temperature stresses unlike those found anywhere else in the United States. To this end, agronomy, soil-nitrogen research, plants-protection research, horticulture, animal science, and forest managements are all pursued.

At a separate unit, a short distance from the main campus, arctic biology studies are being carried out. Under investigation are the musk oxen and reindeer. It is from the musk ox that Qiviut (ke ve oot), an exquisite underbody hair, is obtained. Shearing occurs annually in May. The material is eight times warmer than wool and finer than cashmere. Alaskans have crafted it into various outstanding bits of clothing.

Barley, oats and wheat are now commonly grown in interior Alaska. However, because of its ability to grow to maturity at cool temperatures during short growing season, barley appears most adapted to the far-north. Accordingly, at Delta Junction, 100 miles/166.6km east of Fairbanks, 85,000 acres of barley are under development. This is destined to become feed for livestock in Alaska and for export abroad.

University Avenue is crossed as the campus is left behind. Before entering the Fairbanks yards of the Alaska Railroad, a small wooden trestle is traversed, followed by a 125ft/38m thru-truss bridge. The mainline then negotiates an "S" curve to run parallel to a seven track yard. The yard is 1mi/1.6km long and has a capacity for 478 cars. Just as this yard is passed, a second 1mi/1.6km long yard unfolds. Here the facilities for loading and unloading TOFC/COFC, service and maintenance shops, and additional storage tracks are located. It is from this section of the yard that the Eielson branch deviates to the north and then proceeds for 23mi/38.3km toward the southeast, terminating at Eilson Air Force Base. On the south side of this yard is a recently constructed "balloon" return track. It replaces a "Y" and is used to reverse the direction (with one movement) of the summer passenger train and other rolling stock. This train arrives at the depot on a single track, stub extension, of the mainline. It then backs out of the depot and proceeds down to the loop ultimately reversing itself with the completion of the turn. Next day it backs into the depot again, picks up passengers and is ready to proceed, straight away, to Denali Park and Anchorage.

Numerous other spur tracks leave in all directions from the yard to serve a multitude of business enterprises. This translates into a traffic flow of approximately 1500 cars a week.

As the modest yards disappear, the train lurches sharply to the south as it traverses one of the sharpest curves on the line. Steel wheels pressing on steel rail brings out a distinctive ear piercing screech—then it stops. It's M.P.-470.3, Fairbanks Station, the northern terminus of the line, and the end of the main-line of the northernmost point of any railroad in North America.

Fairbanks

Situated along the banks of the Chena River, near its confluence with the Tanana River, Fairbanks dominates the Tanana Valley. Known as the "Heart of the Golden North", its 65,000 residents live in harmony with its gold rush past and the growing stresses of its present, as it prepares for the future. Fairbank's future will, in part, be realized through the efforts of its greatest asset, the University of Alaska. Situated a short distance to the west, at College, the University spearheads the search for and comprehension of the scientific truths of the north. Already a better life is being realized through this work, not only for man, but for all living things.

The vast majority of Fairbankans are involved, directly or indirectly, with governmental functions such as the military, administrative services and research endeavors. Increasingly, however, mining, lumbering, and agriculture (barley) have come on the scene. While gold and a vast store of varied minerals await "harvesting", oil delivery from the North Slope of the Brooks Range, and oil exploration in the same region, are already realities. Working in conjunction with this endeavor is the MAPCO Oil Refinery at North Pole. In addition Fairbanks serves—by road, water (Nenana) and air—as the distribution center for the west and north of Alaska, an area greater than the whole state of Texas.

Intercontinental flights are using the facilities at the Fairbanks International Airport to a greater degree than ever before.

Uniquely, Fairbanks with its modest population, contains educational, cultural, economic, service, and transportation facilities to a degree unimaginable by any other community of comparable size. While it has had many "boom" cycles, it has never relapsed into a "bust" and become a ghost town. Rather, with each decade the base population has increased, and with it an Alaskan entity. With this evolution not only have the character and needs of this specific community changed, but also those of the interglobal society of which it is a part. Therefore, as the natural resources of the world become depleted, Alaska's natural wealth will become an even more vital necessity. The present role of the Alaska Railroad will change too, so that the present "end of steel" will become the "beginning of steel." To this potential end, a survey line has already been plotted to the Canadian border. Ultimately, the banshee wail of the Alaska Railroad will be heard north of the Alaska Range. This time heading in a southeasterly direction from Fairbanks to the Canadian border, in route at last, by rail, to the United States.

CONCLUSION

As with the cyclic nature of life, the end is just the beginning. So it is with this presentation, for it is in fact the beginning of a new volume. Time evokes changes, creates new horizons, presents new perspectives. Volume Two, therefore, will relate to the entire Alaska Railroad with emphasis on that magnificent line to Seward. For now, our journey has come to an end. On this trip, this is the last stop. All passengers please leave the train. Check the forth-coming timetable for the next train to Anchorage and Seward!

NORTHBOUND FREIGHT, Broad Pass. Note frozen snow and ice on roof of boxcar which is a converted World War II troop carrier. Talkeetna mountains are in the background.

APPROACHING SUMMIT, M.P.-312.5, along the shore of Summit Lake. Southbound passenger train parallels Talkeetna mountains.

SOUTHBOUND COAL TRAIN near Summit; northbound oil train at south end of Broad Pass.

COAL TRAIN approaching Broad Pass section house. Hopper cars are used to transport gravel in the summer from Palmer to Anchorage.

COAL TRAIN southbound, Broad Pass.

SOUTHBOUND PASSENGER TRAIN on isthmus between two lakes at the north end of Broad Pass.

RDC IS ENGULFED by the enormity of Broad Pass. Alaska Range is to the
north (left) and the Talkeetna mountains are to the south (right).

REFLECTION of passenger
train along Summit Lake.

SOUTHBOUND passenger
train near Edes Lake.

NORTHBOUND PASSENGER TRAIN just passing the Broad Pass section
house and entering the tiaga/tundra complex.

RDC in Broad Pass during the development of a spring storm.

DOUBLE UNIT RDC in Broad Pass in the fall.

SUMMIT M.P. – 312.5
ELEVATION 2,363 ft. / 720.2 m.

—Ⓝ→

RDC PARALLELING Summit Lake, Broad Pass, in the fall.

MULTIPLE UNIT oil train approaching the highest summit (2360ft/719.5m) along the Alaska Railroad—but yet the lowest summit crossing in the Rocky Mountains.

SUNSET ON THE TALKEETNA MOUNTAINS at the south end of Broad Pass
casts its reflection on the northbound freight train.

SOUTHBOUND FREIGHT in similar location descending down to Cantwell.

SOUTHBOUND FREIGHT train climbing up the grade from Cantwell, M.P.-319.5, on its way to summit, M.P..312.5.

72

NORTHBOUND FREIGHT kicks up the snow north of Summit Lake just as the sunset turns the white landscape a faint pink.

SOUTHBOUND FREIGHT approaching the village of Cantwell; M.P.-319.5. Reindeer Hills are in the background.

K.A. SMITH, Terminal Superintendent Fairbanks, throwing a switch at Cantwell.

CANTWELL M.P. - 319.5

NORTHBOUND FREIGHT, Cantwell; M.P.-319.5. Peak of Reindeer Hills to the right.

SOUTHBOUND COAL TRAIN, north end of Windy; M.P.-326.7.

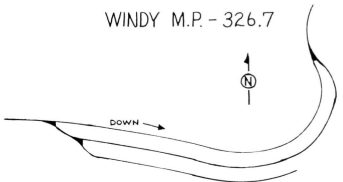

WINDY M.P. - 326.7

DOWN →

CARLO M.P. - 334.4

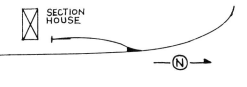

SECTION
HOUSE

—Ⓝ—▶

NORTHBOUND EMPTY COAL TRAIN skirting the boundary of Denali National Park, near Carlo; M.P.-334.4.

OLIVER M.P.-342.7

PASSING SIDING FOR PASSENGER TRAINS

WORK TRAIN, Oliver siding; M.P.-342.7. This is the location of the daily passenger meet, in the summer.

SOUTHBOUND passenger train near Lagoon.

SOUTHBOUND PASSENGER TRAIN with the outer range, of the Alaska range, in the background.

79

PASSENGER TRAIN skirting one of the many lakes near Lagoon.

ALASKA RANGE humbles a passing passenger train.

NORTHBOUND PASSENGER TRAIN leaving Lagoon in preparation for its stop at the Denali National Park Station.

DERELICT RDC being assisted by a G.P.-9 road switcher.

STUNTED GROWTH of diminutive spruce bare testimony to Alaska's harsh winters.

SOUTHBOUND PASSENGER TRAIN approximately 3 mi./5 km. south of
Denali Park Station. Sugarloaf Mountain in the background.

SOUTHBOUND LOCOMOTIVE at the base of Mt. Fellows.

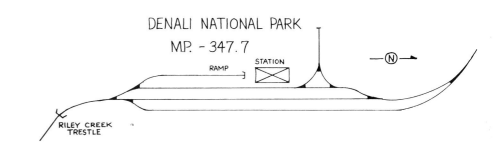

RDC a short distance from Riley Creek.

SOUTHBOUND PASSENGER train entering a cut just after having traversed the Riley Creek bridge.

85

DOUBLE UNIT RDC southbound just south of Denali National Park Station. Geologically older Outer Range of the Alaska Range in the background.

NORTHBOUND PASSENGER TRAIN nearing national park entrance.

MT. FELLOWS appears to act as an obstruction as southbound passenger
climbs out of national park station.

NORTHBOUND PASSENGER TRAIN about to cross Riley Creek trestle at edge
of Denali National Park Station.

A RIOT OF FALL COLOR embraces southbound passenger train as it gingerly crosses Riley Creek trestle. View is looking toward the east.

SPECTACULAR LIGHTING EFFECT of momentary sun, and rock, as north-bound passenger approaches Riley Creek trestle. Denali National Park Station, M.P.-347.7 rests approximately 150 yds./136.8 m. north of the trestle.

91

SOUTHBOUND COAL TRAIN pulling 65 loaded coal cars, 80 tons each, over the Riley Creek trestle.

WESTERLY VIEW of Riley Creek trestle. "Bush", RDC enroute to pick up hikers, campers and wilderness travelers.

HINES CREEK with Riley Creek trestle. Southbound passenger train over-shadowed by Mt. Fellows.

PANORAMIC VIEW of Denali National Park Station and visitors complex.
Southbound passenger train shortly after leaving the station.

SOUTHBOUND MIXED FREIGHT train leaving Denali National Park Station,
RDC in the distance, just prior to leaving for local service to the south.
Sugarloaf Mountain in the background.

SOUTHBOUND FREIGHT train slowly passing by Denali National Park Station.

NORTHBOUND PASSENGER train meet with southbound RDC at Denali National Park Station. Fang Mountain in the distance.

A RIOT OF COLOR embraces southbound passenger train a short distance from the Denali National Park station. Mt. Healy dominates the scene. Photo by Bernice Deely.

NORTHBOUND PASSENGER TRAIN at M.P.-349.7 on a ledge high above the Nenana River.

RDC NEGOTIATING(very gingerly) the uncertain shoulders of the Nenana River Canyon.

SOUTHBOUND RDC on a continuous climb to summit. Scene is located approximately at M.P.-350, in the Nenana River Canyon.

SOUTHBOUND PASSENGER TRAIN crossing the high trestle on the shoulder of Mt. Healy.

F.P.-7 heading southbound, passenger train at M.P.-350.

PANORAMIC OVERVIEW of the southfaced Mt. Healy complex. Southbound passenger train clings precipitously to the mountain shoulder. Photo by Bernice Deely.

A PANORAMA of overwhelming mountain scenery dominates what appears to be a model railroad train.

MT. HEALY with its Matterhorn appearance humbles the southbound passenger train at M.P.-350.5.

THE OUTER RANGE of the Alaska Range overshadows a northbound freight.

NORTHBOUND PASSENGER TRAIN complements Sugarloaf Mountain to the east; M.P.-351.4.

RDC in the winter crossing a wooden trestle with frozen stream below at
M.P.-351.4.

SOUTHBOUND PASSENGER TRAIN crosses a fissure on the shoulder of the Outer Range over a wooden trestle.

NORTHBOUND PASSENGER TRAIN about to enter rock-bound Nenana River Canyon paralleling its frozen river.

SOUTHBOUND PASSENGER TRAIN at south end of Nenana River Canyon.

NORTHBOUND TRAIN emerging from north portal of the curved Moody Tunnel, Nenana River Canyon.

SOUTHBOUND FREIGHT emerging from south portal of curved, Moody Tunnel.

NORTHBOUND COAL TRAIN entering south portal of the curved Moody Tunnel high above the Nenana River.

112

NORTHBOUND PASSENGER TRAIN coming into Garner, M.P.-355.7, situated at the north end of the Nenana River Canyon.

NORTHBOUND PASSENGER TRAIN at Garner; M.P.-355.7.

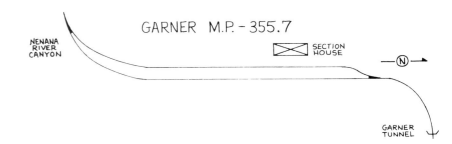

DRAMATIC VIEW of southbound passenger train snaking along the Nenana River Canyon not far from Healy.

FROZEN NENANA RIVER Canyon cradles a southbound freight train emerging from a deep cut in its walls.

A SHORT DISTANCE from Healy a southbound passenger train proceeds along
its extremely circuitous route along the north end of the Nenana River Canyon.

HIGH ABOVE the Nenana River the daily passenger train to Denali National Park provides awe inspiring views for its dome seated passengers.

COAL TRAIN at similar location, at M.P.-356.8.

SOUTHBOUND PASSENGER TRAIN proceeding along a U shaped curve as it
enters the north end of the Nenana River Canyon.
The flats of Healy Creek are seen in the background.

VOLCANIC ROCK and ash in colors of pink, orange, red and white, provide a collage of background color for this northbound passenger train just south of Healy.

SIMILAR LOCATION as above photo. Note lignite seams to the far right of the photo.

A RIOT OF COLOR complements the passenger train at the north end of the
Nenana River Canyon. The Outer Range of the Alaska Range dwarfs the train.

COAL TRAIN at Healy; M.P.- 358.7.

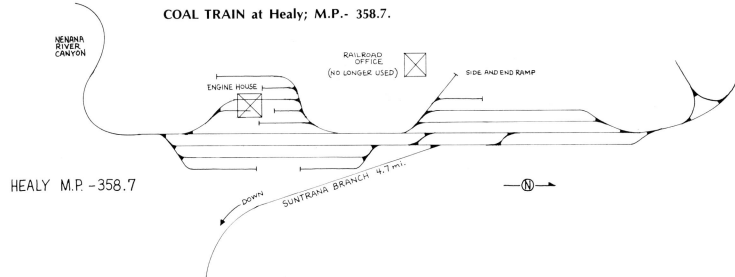

NENANA
RIVER
CANYON

RAILROAD
OFFICE
(NO LONGER USED)

SIDE AND END RAMP

ENGINE HOUSE

HEALY M.P. -358.7

DOWN

SUNTRANA BRANCH 4.7 mi.

—Ⓝ—➤

122

MIXED FREIGHT TRAIN proceeding to Fairbanks at Sunset from the Healy yards.

COAL TRAIN at Healy preparing to leave the yards enroute to Clear, Fairbanks and Eielson Air Force Base.

COAL TRAIN with Bicentennial caboose in Healy yards.

NORTHBOUND FREIGHT not far from the Usibelli Tipple; M.P.-362.3.

COAL TRAIN on Suntrana branch out of Healy. The branch was used in the past as an active coal feeder; now it is only used during emergencies for hopper loading.

FAIRBANKS coal train leaving Healy.

OWL ARRIVING in Healy, bound for Anchorage.

COAL TRAIN on Usibelli spur heading for the Usibelli Tipple, M.P.-362.3, for subsequent loading.

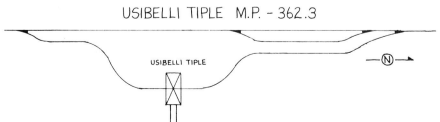

LEAD LOCOMOTIVEon Fairbanks coal train passing Usibelli Tipple.

HOPPER CARS slowly passing under the tipple, in constant movement, while being loaded.

IN THE WINTER, prior to being loaded, hopper cars are sprayed with anti-freeze to prevent the coal from freezing to the car sides.

FAIRBANKS COAL TRAIN on the main line shortly after being loaded at the Usibelli Tipple.

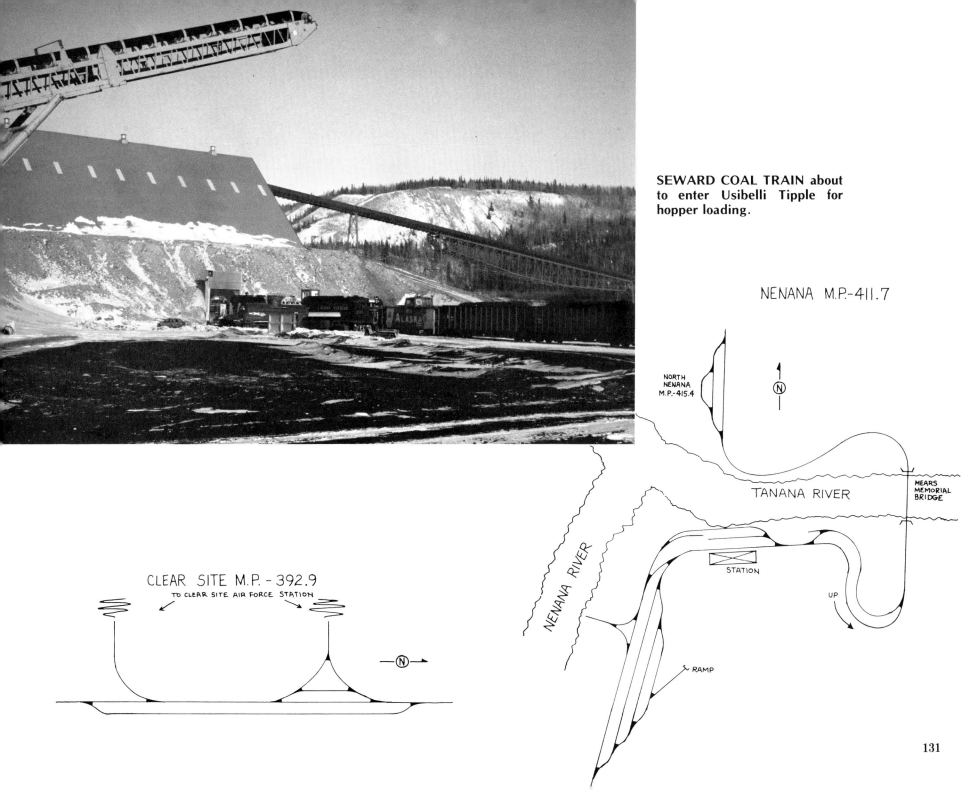

SEWARD COAL TRAIN about to enter Usibelli Tipple for hopper loading.

NENANA M.P.-411.7

NORTH NENANA M.P.-415.4

TANANA RIVER

MEARS MEMORIAL BRIDGE

NENANA RIVER

STATION

UP

RAMP

CLEAR SITE M.P. - 392.9

TO CLEAR SITE AIR FORCE STATION

132

ANCHORAGE BOUND freight train passing over the frozen Tanana River on the Mears Memorial Bridge. In the foreground is an Indian fishwheel commonly found on the Tanana and Yukon Rivers.

WEEKLY RDC passing stored tug boats banked along the Nenana River at its confluence with the Yukon River at Nenana; M.P.-411.7.

PASSENGER TRAIN passing over the Tanana River on the Mears Memorial
Bridge. Train is southbound and the view is from east to west.

FAIRBANKS BOUND passenger train climbing to the approaches of the Mears Memorial Bridge. Alaska Range looms in the distance.

135

ANCHORAGE BOUND passenger train passing old Indian caches, Nenana; M.P.-411.7.

FREIGHT TRAIN passing the famous St. Marks Episcopal Mission, Nenana.

FAIRBANKS PASSENGER TRAIN crossing the Tanana River over the Mears Memorial Bridge.

PANORAMIC VIEW of the Tanana River-Nenana complex. Barges are being loaded while a southbound passenger train passes through the town.

FREIGHT TRAIN passing Nenana Ice Classic office. Wedged in between is a replica of the famous Ice Classic tripod.

EMPTY SOUTHBOUND COAL TRAIN passing Nenana Ice Classic office.

LOOKING FROM THE WEST at the Nenana passenger station and docks while a southbound passenger train stops to pick up a group of Indian travelers.

COAL TRAIN destined for the Usibelli Tipple stopping at Nenana for confirmation of orders.

PASSING FREIGHT TRAIN at Dome, M.P.-456.2, the northern most point on the Alaska Railroad.

DOME M.P. - 456.2

FAIRBANKS PASSENGER TRAIN approaching Sheep Creek Road just a short distance from its final destination.

143

UNIVERSITY OF ALASKA, Fairbanks Farm complex, paralleling the Alaska Railroad in College.

SOUTHBOUND empty coal train passing through College.

FLOWER FIELDS, University of Alaska, along the railroad right-of-way.

ARCTIC FOX express container train to Anchorage passing a field of barley.

EXCURSION TRAIN about to leave the Fairbanks yard during an early autumn snowfall.

DENALI NATIONAL PARK passenger train passing on a truss bridge over the Noyes Slough. Fairbanks yard is located just east of the bridge.

TRAILER BEING LOADED onto a flatcar in the Fairbanks yard.

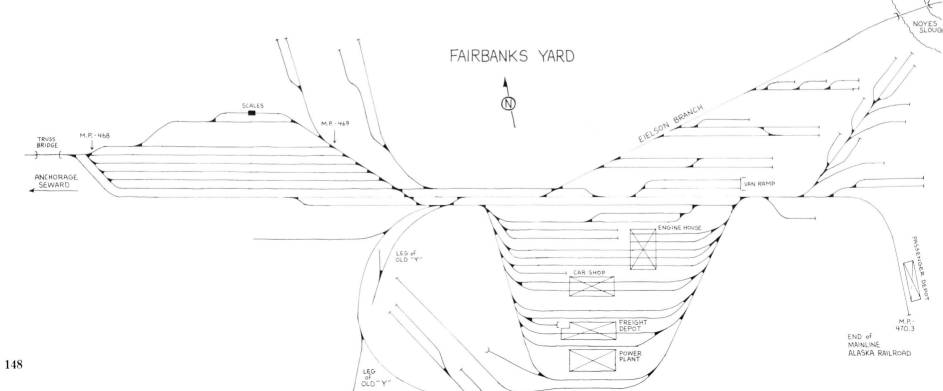

FAIRBANKS YARD

N

SCALES

M.P. - 468

M.P. - 469

TRUSS
BRIDGE

ANCHORAGE
SEWARD

EIELSON BRANCH

VAN RAMP

NOYES
SLOUGH

ENGINE HOUSE

LEG of
OLD "Y"

CAR SHOP

FREIGHT
DEPOT

POWER
PLANT

LEG
of
OLD "Y"

PASSENGER DEPOT

M.P. -
470.3

END of
MAINLINE
ALASKA RAILROAD

SWITCHER SHUNTING CARS in the Fairbanks yard.

ARCTIC FOX waiting for its call to proceed on its overnight run to Anchorage. A switcher stands by waiting for the Arctic Fox to clear the main line so that it may resume its work. The red herald on the nose of the switcher is a hold over from the days when the railroad was under the control of the U.S. Department of Transportation. The railroad is now owned by the State of Alaska.

149

PASSENGERS, YOUNG AND OLD, boarding an RDC at the Fairbanks station in the early morning hours.

OPEN HOUSE to the public is sponsored periodically by the Alaska Railroad.

TOURIST PASSENGERS, in front of Fairbanks station, preparing to board passenger train destined for Denali National Park.

THE END of the main line in Fairbanks; M.P.-470.3.

152

TYPICAL FAIRBANKS STATION SCENE in the summer. Alaska's flag, the Big Dipper and the North Star, has been painted on the side of the Holland America Line, Westours, luxury passenger dome car.

PILE DRIVER repairing small wooden trestle near M.P.-351.2.

ARTICULATED FLAT CARS for TOFC/COFC transport.

Equipment Roster

UNIQUE COAL HAULING hopper cars passing through Broad Pass. In the summer, when the demand for coal diminishes, these cars are used to haul gravel in the Anchorage area.

EQUIPMENT ROSTER—ALASKA RAILROAD

LOCOMOTIVES

1800 Series, EMD, GP-7-1800 HP	7
2000 Series, EMD, GP-32-2-2000 HP	8
2500 Series, EMD, GP-35-2500 HP	3
2800 Series, EMD, GP-49-2800 HP	9
3000 Series, EMD, GP-40-2-3000 HP	21
TOTAL	**48**

BOX CARS
(8 Hi-Cube) — 108

GONDOLAS
(50 and 70 ton) — 260

FLAT CARS — 381

FLAT CARS (leased) — 150

ARTICULATED FLAT CARS
(3 units to a car) — 43

BALLAST CARS
(Multi-Service) — 78

PASSENGER CARS

Chair	9
Dome Chair	3
Diner	2
Counter Cafe	2
Baggage	4
Steam Power	2
Electric Power	1
Business Car (Denali)	1
Full Dome Cars (Holland-American Line and Princess Tours)	10
TOTAL	**34**

RDC 3 — 5

SHIPPING PLATFORMS — 83

UNIT RAIL BOXES — 199

HEATING UNITS — 262

REFRIGERATOR CARS — 10

COVERED HOPPERS — 19

ALASKA RAILROAD'S special grain cars enroute to the United States and Canada for use in seasonal traffic in those regions.

LOADED hopper cars passing through Windy; M.P.-326.7.

GENERAL MOTORS, E-8, passenger locomotive in the Fairbanks Yard. This unit and all other F units have been sold to other railroads.

CLOSE UP of Alaska Railroad grain car.

HOPPERS (Twin)	1
HOPPERS (Quad)	56
HOPPERS (State Owned)	20
TANK CARS	
ARR	61
North Pole Refinery (leased)	179
Chevron Oil (leased)	33
Tesoro-Alaska Petroleum (leased)	18
Texaco Inc. (leased)	15
Van Gas, Inc. (leased)	5
U.S. Army (DODX)	100
POWER CARS (Freight)	7
CABOOSES	21
AIR DUMP CARS	44
LOCOMOTIVE CRANES	11
SNOW PLOWS (Rotary)	1
SPREADERS (Jordan)	2

TANK-TRAIN passing through Broad Pass.

MOOSE CREEK trestle on the Eielson Air Force branch at Sunset. The Alaska Range in the background is over 100 mi./ 166.6 km. away.

RDC, southbound emerging from south portal of Garner tunnel; M.P.-355.7.

TOUR ALASKA, full length dome car and its happy passengers approaching Denali National Park station.

TOUR ALASKA as seen from a cliff high above the railroad.

DAVE THUMMA, Eskimo engineer, Alaska Railroad, about to start another run.

THE WARMTH and friendliness of the Alaska Railroad and its employees is personified by this passing conductor.

SOUTHBOUND PASSENGER TRAIN winding through the mountains of the Denali National Park, at M.P.-333.5. Northward flowing Nenana River in the foreground.